The Healing Power of The SACRAMENTS

The Healing Power of the SACRAMENTS

Jim McManus C.SS.R.

ST PAULS

Permissions and Acknowledgments:

Unless otherwise noted, all scripture quotations in this work are taken from the *Good News Bible,* the *Bible in Today's English Version.* Copyright American Bible Society, 1976. Used by permission. For the United Kingdom, permission to retain the American edition is grnted by the Britishnd Foreign Bible Society and Collins Publishing, London, joint publishers of the British usge edition.

Excerpts from *The Documents of Vatican II* are reprinted with permission of Americ Press, Inc., 106 West 56 Street, New York, NY 10019.

Excerpts from the English translation of *The Roman Missal* © 1973, International Committee on English in the Liturgy, Inc. (ICEL); excerpts from the English translation of the *Rite of Penance* © 1974, ICEL; excerpts from the English translation of *Pastoral Care of the sick: Rites of Anointing and Viaticum* © 1982, ICEL. All rights reserved.

Specified extracts from *How People Change* by Allen Wheelis, Copyright 1973 by Allen Wheelis. By permission of Harper & Row, Publishers, Inc.

_____

Cum Permissu Superiorum

This Indian Edition by permission of Ave Maria Press. Notre Dame. Indiana 46556, U.S.A.

For sale in India only.

ISBN 81-7109-048-6

Cover : *Katherine A. Robinson*

Text design : *Elizabeth French*

ST PAULS is an activity
of priests and brothers of the Society of St Paul
who proclaim the Gospel
through the media of social communication.

Printed by J. Njarakkatt at St Paul Press Training School.
Nagasandra, Bangalore and published by
ST PAULS, Bandra, Mumbai 400 050
1996

TO MY MOTHER
with love and gratitude

CONTENTS

Foreword

During the Second Vatican Council and since then, Catholic theology's dominant idea-symbol for the church has been the biblical one of the Body of Christ.

The concept is present and even dominates the Council's doctrine on the church. The Second Vatican Council sees the church as identified with the risen Jesus, as in a mysterious union with him risen, a union that is even a kind of identification; the church *is* the Body of the risen Christ.

As his Body, the church acts as the extension of the incarnation, as the prolongation of Jesus' life on earth. Because the church is a living Body, organic, filled with life, it changes in history. As Jesus did, the church grows in age and grace and wisdom. And, like any living thing, the church suffers. In this world we belong not yet to the church triumphant but to the church militant, the church suffering, wounded, under attack, always falling and rising again. The church finds herself in the structure of the cross.

Because the church acts as the extension in our history of Jesus Christ, as his Body, it is—as he became at his incarnation—fully embedded, incarnate, in the human material world. Not merely a voice announcing the gospel, not just a collection of people, the church is a Body, and it functions in a down-to-earth, human, concrete way: through her ministers and through all her members, and in a special way through her sacraments.

Jesus still speaks, acts, and heals through his Body, the church; he speaks and acts and heals in a special and especially efficacious way through the sacraments of the church. The sacraments are the church's hands, the hands of Christ's Body, the hands of Jesus reaching out to touch us and to heal us.

The church's sacraments bring us the Lord's salvation. But salvation is not only for the world to come. Jesus came not only to call us to conversion and to get us to heaven and to eternal life with the Father and with himself. He came to give us life now in this world, the life of his Holy Spirit welling up inside us. This life heals us, spiritually and psychologically and even physically—because it affects us as persons in our entire being, spiritual and psychological and physical.

Jesus did not stop healing when he died. He rose, and he still ministers healing to us through the healing hands of his Body, the church.

What does that mean in practice? What is the significance, in pastoral terms, of the healing function of the sacraments?

In *The Healing Power of the Sacraments*, James McManus answers these questions in a clear and practical way, opening up to us the meaning of the fact that the Lord heals us through the sacraments. But, of course, the book does not stop there. The Lord heals us not only through the sacraments but also through our prayers for and with one another, through our prayers together; and he heals each of us through our own personal prayer and daily lived-out union with him.

The Lord calls us to pray together and to pray with and for one another. And this prayer together and for

one another is healing prayer. We can pray specifically
for healing. But, even when we do not, even when our
prayer is general or for intentions other than healing, it
has a healing dimension; it helps to heal us, to make us
whole. In this way, through prayer, we bring the
Lord's healing to one another.

The teaching of this book comes out of Father
McManus' broad and deep pastoral experience. Many
readers will have, as I have, already received healing
grace through his ministry. And all of us can receive
the Lord's healing grace now, through reading and
praying over and acting on what James McManus has
written for us.

                                    Robert Faricy, S.J.

Preface

One day in 1936 our family doctor told my mother that my father would not live through the night. He was suffering from pneumonia, and there were no antibiotics in those days. The doctor could do nothing to prolong his life.

My mother, who knew that only God could save my father, sent word to Father Ignatius at the Passionist monastery near Enniskillen requesting that he pray for my father's healing. Father Ignatius, a parish missioner, was well-known for praying with the sick. He sent word to my mother that my father would not die. When the doctor called the next day, my father was fully conscious and recovering from his illness. He lived for another 26 years.

That healing took place two years before I was born. The knowledge that God restored my father through the prayers of Father Ignatius has always been with me and has frequently challenged my own lack of faith. I owe my very existence to my mother's faith in divine healing. This book is my thanks to God for that faith and for that healing.

The Healing Power of the Sacraments could not have been written without the cooperation of many people. Sister Laetitia typed the first draft. My confreres Bill Brereton, Oliver Keyes and John Shannon read the original manuscript and made helpful corrections and suggestions. Beverly Ahearn read the final draft and made further helpful suggestions.

Father Bob Faricy, S.J., my mentor in the Christian Spirituality Program at Creighton University, encouraged me to seek publication. I wish also to acknowledge my indebtedness to Ed McDonough, Francis MacNutt, Dennis and Matthew Linn, and Bob de Grandis. I have learned from their teaching and received abundantly through their ministry. My gratitude also to the Reverend John Richards and the ecumenical Inner Healing Gathering which he hosts once a year. Likewise, my thanks to consultant psychiatrist John Mathai who hosted an inner healing group in our monastery in Perth.

My best teachers, however, were the men and women who came to me for prayer and the sacraments and who shared with me how the Lord had worked in their lives to heal them. Without this sharing and without their testimonies, I would not have been able to write this book. My special thanks to them.

Jim McManus, C.SS.R.

ONE:
The Healing Ministry of Jesus

God "will cause the bright dawn of salvation to rise on us." With these prophetic words Zechariah, the father of John the Baptist, proclaimed the Lord's coming. Jesus brings into this world everything that God is in himself. He brings love, compassion, kindness and mercy. He manifests in himself the very nature of God.

In Jesus Christ we see manifest in human nature the whole mystery of God. Psalm 23 tells us, "The Lord is merciful and loving." Jesus is the incarnation of that mercy and love. The Lord, the psalm continues, "is full of constant love." Jesus is the visible manifestation of that constant love. When his disciple Philip asked Jesus, "Lord, show us the Father; that is all we need," Jesus replied, "Whoever has seen me has seen the Father."

In our reflections on the healing ministry of Jesus we must never lose sight of this basic truth: In observing the works of Jesus we are seeing the Father at work. Jesus said,

> "I do nothing on my own authority, but I say only what the Father has instructed me to say. And he who sent me is with me; he has not left me alone, because I always do what pleases him" (Jn 8:28-29).

Every work of Jesus is pleasing in the sight of God;

13

every time Jesus heals the sick we see a work which pleases the Father. St. Peter summed up the life and ministry of Jesus in this way:

> He went everywhere, doing good and healing all who were under the power of the Devil, for God was with him (Acts 10:38).

Ministry in the Power of the Spirit

The people of Nazareth, where Jesus grew up, were intrigued when Jesus began to preach and teach and heal. They wanted to know where he got his power and his knowledge.

> Then Jesus went to Nazareth, where he had been brought up, and on the Sabbath he went as usual to the synagogue. He stood up to read the Scriptures and was handed the book of the prophet Isaiah. He unrolled the scroll and found the place where it is written,
>
> "The Spirit of the Lord is upon me,
> because he has chosen me to bring good news to the poor.
> He has sent me to proclaim liberty to the captives
>   and recovery of sight to the blind,
> to set free the oppressed
>   and announce that the time has come
> when the Lord will save his people."
>
> Jesus rolled up the scroll, gave it back to the attendant, and sat down. All the people in the synagogue had their eyes fixed on him, as he said to them, "This passage of scripture has come true today, as you heard it being read" (Lk 4:16-21).

To the people who wondered how their carpenter could have become a prophet, Jesus said, "The Spirit of the Lord is upon me." Jesus attributed all his work, all his ministry to the Spirit. Let us ponder how the Spirit came to rest on Jesus:

> After all the people had been baptized, Jesus also was baptized. While he was praying, heaven was opened, and the Holy Spirit came down upon him in bodily form like a dove. And a voice came from heaven, "You are my own dear Son. I am pleased with you" (Lk 3:21-22).

Luke presents the scene very carefully. All the people have been baptized by John; Jesus too has been baptized. And now Jesus is alone in prayer. It is on the praying Jesus that God pours out his Spirit. Luke continues:

> Jesus returned from the Jordan full of the Holy Spirit and was led by the Spirit into the desert, where he was tempted by the Devil for forty days (Lk 4:1-2).

Notice Jesus' response to the gift of the Spirit: He allows himself to be led. He surrenders his whole life to the Father so that the Spirit can lead him in doing the Father's will. Without this act of surrender, the Spirit cannot lead. The sign of being led by the Spirit is doing the Father's will. After his 40 days in the desert, where he prayed and fasted and was tempted by the Devil, Jesus began his public ministry and "the power of the Holy Spirit was with him."

Luke has highlighted three phases in Jesus' experience of the Spirit:

Jesus full of the Spirit
    The Father's free gift, given to Jesus as he prays.

Jesus led by the Spirit
    Jesus' response to the Father's gift. Without this response of surrender, the Spirit could not lead.

Jesus in the power of the Spirit
> The Spirit empowers Jesus to do the works of
> God. His ministry begins.

It is important for us to see the ministry of Jesus in the light of his experience of the Spirit. His whole ministry is in the power of the Spirit. Outside that power of the Spirit there is no ministry. Jesus came in human weakness.

> . . . he gave up all he had,
> and took the nature of a servant.
> He became like man (Phil 2:7).

He didn't have in himself the power to heal or proclaim the gospel. This power came to him from the Holy Spirit. That is why Luke spends so much time retelling the story of Jesus' baptism and his response to the gift of the Spirit.

Jesus not only received the Spirit, but he also heard the words: "You are my own dear Son. I am pleased with you." Jesus was aware of himself as the one chosen by God, the beloved Son anointed with the Holy Spirit and sent to bring the good news that the reign of Satan was ended and the reign of God was at hand. James Dunn expresses this truth:

> The eschatological kingdom was present for Jesus
> because the eschatological Spirit was present in and
> through him. In other words, it was not so much a
> case of "Where I am there is the kingdom," as,
> "Where the Spirit is there is the kingdom." It was
> the manifestation of the power of God which was
> the sign of the kingdom.[1]

---

[1] James Dunn, *Jesus and the Spirit: A Study of the Religious and Charismatic Experience of Jesus and the First Christians As Reflected in the New Testament* (Philadelphia: The Westminster Press, 1979).

Jesus himself responded to those who accused him of working through the power of Satan:

> "You say that I drive out demons because Beelzebul gives me the power to do so. . . . No, it is not Beelzebul, but God's Spirit, who gives me the power to drive out demons, which proves that the Kingdom of God has already come upon you" (Mt 12:27-28).

Jesus, in his human weakness, had no power to drive out demons. Often we ignore this truth and attribute all his great works to the power which he had as Son of God. To the question, "How did Jesus cast out demons?" we frequently get the reply, "Jesus cast out demons because he was the Son of God." But Jesus never made that claim; he said that it was through the Spirit of God that he cast out demons. He preached that the kingdom of God was at hand, and he was saying that the power which the Spirit gave to him over evil spirits was a proof that his preaching was true.

Preachers today should ask themselves what proof they offer that "the kingdom of God is at hand." Jesus proved that his preaching was true by pointing to what the Spirit was doing in him. And Jesus proves that the preaching of his disciples is true by giving them his Spirit.

> After the Lord Jesus had talked with them, he was taken up to heaven and sat at the right side of God. The disciples went and preached everywhere, and the Lord worked with them and proved that their preaching was true by the miracles that were performed (Mk 16:19-20).

St. Paul tells us how he preached the gospel:

> We brought the Good News to you, not with words
> only, but also with power and the Holy Spirit, and
> with complete conviction of its truth (1 Thes 1:5)

Just as the ministry of Jesus was in the power of the
Spirit, so too the ministry of his disciples is in the same
power. There are not two ministries, the ministry of
Jesus and the ministry of his disciples. There is only
one ministry, and that is the ministry of Jesus in the
power of the Spirit which Jesus now shares with us.
This truth is very clearly expressed in the words of the
Fourth Eucharistic Prayer:

> And that we might live no longer for ourselves but
>   for him,
> he sent the Holy Spirit from you, Father,
> as his first gift to those who believe,
> to complete his work on earth
> and bring us the fullness of grace.

Jesus' whole ministry was in the power of the
Spirit. He cast out demons through the power of the
Spirit; in the same way, it was through the power of
the Spirit that he healed the sick.

> One day when Jesus was teaching, some Pharisees
> and teachers of the Law were sitting there who had
> come from every town in Galilee and Judea and
> from Jerusalem. The power of the Lord was present
> for Jesus to heal the sick (Lk 5:17).

The phrase "the power of the Lord" means "the Spirit
of the Lord." Again we must reflect that since Jesus
became like us in all things but sin, since he really took
on all our human weakness, he did not have the power
to heal in himself. That power came to him through
the Holy Spirit. When we see Jesus healing the sick we
see the Spirit of God at work. And if the Spirit of God
is at work, the reign of God has begun. When the

disciples of John the Baptist came to Jesus to ask whether he really was the Christ, Jesus said to them:

> "Go back and tell John what you are hearing and seeing: the blind can see, the lame can walk, those who suffer from dreaded skin diseases are made clean, the deaf hear, the dead are brought back to life, and the Good News is preached to the poor" (Mt 11:4-5).

Schnackenburg comments:

> The testimony of Jesus to himself makes it obvious how closely his miracles and preaching are related. The point of the cures is to prove what he is proclaiming, the all-embracing salvific will of God: they are signs of the eschatological salvation which has come with Jesus. It was already there, in so far as the blind actually see, the deaf hear, the lame walk, the lepers are cleansed. It was not yet completely there, in so far as sicknesses are not yet healed and the whole accursed earth not yet transfigured. It is precisely this salvation, perceptible already though not yet fulfilled, that is dawning with the reign of God manifested in these cures and wonders.[2]

The miracles of healing are signs of the reign of God. Notice that modern scholars prefer to speak of *the reign of God* when referring to the present, and they keep the term *the kingdom of God* for referring to the future. The kingdom of God has yet to come, but the reign of God has already begun. God reigns through his Spirit in the heart of humankind, and the sign of that reign is the overthrow of all the powers of Satan. Exorcism is a sign of God's reign; so also is healing. Both exorcism and healing are signs of the reign of God in the present world of darkness and sin, and at

---

[2] Rudolph Schnackenburg, *God's Rule and Kingdom* (London, 1965).

the same time they foreshadow the complete triumph of God's kingdom in the future:

> For Christ must rule until God defeats all enemies and puts them under his feet. The last enemy to be defeated will be death (1 Cor 15:25-26).

Christ's miracles, then, are signs of the future triumph of God's kingdom. They are not in themselves the presence of the full reality of the kingdom. The last enemy, death, already defeated in Christ, has still to be defeated in us. Jesus did not come to simply banish sickness or suffering or death here and now. He came to establish the reign of God in our hearts, and when God reigns triumphantly in his kingdom among us, his kingdom which is still to come, all sickness and suffering and even death will be abolished. In the meantime, as we say in the Mass, "We wait in joyful hope for the coming of our Savior, Jesus Christ."

> Just as the reign of God has indeed begun but has not reached full deployment, so too Christ's healing activity has indeed broken in but is not completed. The miracles of Jesus are like lights in the night. They show us a way and enable us to hope that eventually we will see the complete light of day of which these are but a single ray.[3]

In the gospel we see Jesus casting out demons through the power of the Spirit. We see him healing the sick through the power of the Spirit. And we are told too that Jesus preached through that same power. Everything that Jesus did—preaching, teaching, healing, exorcising—he did through the power of the Holy Spirit. And he promised that same power to his disciples.

---

[3] Alfons Weiss, *The Miracles of Jesus* (Chicago, 1972).

"When the Holy Spirit comes upon you, you will be filled with power, and you will be witnesses for me in Jerusalem, in all Judea and Samaria, and to the ends of the earth" (Acts 1:8).

Just as Jesus worked through the power of the Holy Spirit, so he expects his disciples to work through that same power. Jesus expects his disciples to continue to do the same works as he himself did and to do even greater works:

"I am telling you the truth: whoever believes in me will do what I do—yes, he will do even greater things, because I am going to the Father" (Jn 14:12).

For a long time I could not really accept these words of Christ. I would say to myself, How can anyone do a greater work than Jesus, the Son of God? I was attributing all the works of Jesus to his divinity. He was divine, and therefore he worked all those miracles; we are only human, so how can we do a greater work than he did? How can we even do the same works that he did? All the time I was missing the central truth revealed in the ministry of Jesus. What he did, he did through the power of the Holy Spirit. And he has given that same Holy Spirit to us.

TWO:
The Place of Suffering in the Christian Life

The good news of Christ is not that there is no longer any sense in or any need for suffering. The good news is that in Christ all suffering can make us obedient children of God. We have Christ himself as our model.

> In his life on earth Jesus made his prayers and requests with loud cries and tears to God, who could save him from death. Because he was humble and devoted, God heard him. But even though he was God's Son, he learned through his sufferings to be obedient (Heb 5: 7-8).

The sign and the proof of Christ's total obedience is his acceptance of his passion and death.

At the approach of his passion Jesus experienced great anguish of soul. He said to his chosen disciples in the Garden of Gethsemane,

> "The sorrow in my heart is so great that it almost crushes me" (Mk 14:34).

To his Father he prayed:

> "Father, . . . if you will, take this cup of suffering away from me. Not my will, however, but your will be done." An angel from heaven appeared to him

and strengthened him. In great anguish he prayed even more fervently; his sweat was like drops of blood falling to the ground (Lk 22:42-44).

God heard the cry of Jesus. He sent an angel, a messenger bringing his own strength, to comfort him. He did not remove the cause of the agony, but he gave Jesus the strength and the power to go through his passion and death. The hour had come. Jesus had longed for this hour, but in his weak human nature he did not have the strength to live through his hour. And so he prayed. He kept vigil in the garden until the Father sent him strength from heaven in the form of the angel. In all the suffering which ensued—his mock trial, his cruel scourging, his carrying of the cross, his agonizing death—we see Jesus sustained by the strength of the Father.

Why did he have to suffer so much? Why did God his Father not release him? These are the very questions with which the scribes and Pharisees taunted him as he hung on the cross:

"He saved others, but he cannot save himself! Isn't he the king of Israel? If he comes down off the cross now, we will believe in him! He trusts in God and claims to be God's Son. Well, then, let us see if God wants to save him now!" (Mt 27:42-43).

The leaders of the people were blind. They acted on the assumption that suffering was a sign of punishment, that God would never allow the good to suffer. Therefore lack of suffering was a sure sign of God's favor. They could not understand the meaning of the cross. Even Jesus' own disciples were shocked and scandalized by his crucifixion. It was as he had warned them,

"This very night all of you will run away and leave me, for the scripture says, 'God will kill the shepherd, and the sheep of the flock will be scattered' " (Mt 26:31).

Jesus faced suffering with complete confidence in God. While praying for deliverance from such dreadful suffering he never once put his own will before the will of the Father. And in his total obedience to the Father's will we see Jesus receiving from the Father the strength and the power to face death.

Jesus teaches us how to face our own sufferings. Christians have been taught by the Spirit to unite themselves with the suffering of Jesus in all trials, and, just as Jesus received strength from his Father to face his agony, so Christians receive strength through their union with Christ to face their sufferings.

"And sorrow, like a sharp sword, will break your heart"

All the disciples were scandalized by the death of Jesus. But his mother was not. She stood near his cross. Artists throughout the ages have tried to express her suffering. We do not know her thoughts or her feelings, but we do know that her love brought her to Calvary.

As we contemplate Mary standing at the foot of the cross, we realize in a new way how the prophecy of Simeon has been fulfilled. When Mary brought the child Jesus to the temple Simeon foretold that she would suffer:

Simeon blessed them and said to Mary, his mother, "This child is chosen by God for the destruction and the salvation of many in Israel. He will be a sign from God which many people will speak against and so reveal their secret thoughts. And sorrow, like a sharp sword, will break your own heart" (Lk 2:34-35).

Contemplation is, perhaps, the only way to understand the meaning and the mystery of suffering. Contemplation is opening our eyes to the mystery of God. Only those whose eyes have been opened by the Lord can contemplate the mystery of God's love in the crucified Christ. Mary's eyes were opened. She contemplated the mystery of God in the word spoken to her by the angel and she said,

> "I am the Lord's servant, may it happen to me as you have said" (Lk 1:38).

She contemplated the mystery in her child, and she pondered in her heart the things that were said about him. And in deep silence she contemplated the mystery of God in her son hanging on the cross. In the garden Jesus had prayed that the Father's will be done. At the foot of his cross Mary continued to pray, "May it happen to me as you have said." The word the Lord spoke to her contained not just the mystery of the conception of her son, but the whole mystery of the incarnation, the mystery of God becoming man and dying for us. Having said yes to the word of the angel, Mary did not have to speak again. Her yes was total. On Calvary she was silent, but her very presence at the foot of the cross filled the whole church with her yes—her yes to God's mystery of salvation and her yes to her vocation to be the mother of the crucified redeemer and the spiritual mother of all the disciples. Mary, God's mother and our mother, was no stranger to suffering. Our whole Catholic tradition teaches us to turn to her in all sorrow and sickness and ask for her powerful intercession.

"Then he opened their minds"

Jesus does not want us to live in ignorance of the meaning of his suffering. His disciples were blind, but he healed them:

> Then he opened their minds to understand the Scriptures, and said to them, "This is what is written: the Messiah must suffer and must rise from death three days later, and in his name the message about repentance and the forgiveness of sins must be preached to all nations, beginning in Jerusalem" (Lk 24:45-47).

Suffering causes not just pain in the body, not just anguish in the soul, but confusion and bewilderment in the mind. We need the Lord to open our minds to the mystery of the cross in our lives. Only then will we be able to enter into the mystery as rational beings and share in that mystery by following him.

> "If anyone wants to come with me, he must forget himself, take up his cross every day, and follow me" (Lk 9:23).

Faced with suffering we must pray like Jesus. We must always bring our suffering, with great simplicity and confidence to the Father, and then we too must pray, "Not my will, but your will be done."

St. Paul clearly understood the mystery of the cross.

> When I came to you, my brothers, to preach God's secret truth, I did not use big words and great learning. For while I was with you, I made up my mind to forget everything except Jesus Christ, and especially his death on the cross (1 Cor 2:1-2).

Paul had received a new insight: The very thing which the world rejects as sheer folly and nonsense is the wisdom of God. Paul boasts:

> As for us, we proclaim the crucified Christ, a
> message that is offensive to the Jews and nonsense to
> the Gentiles; but for those whom God has called,
> both Jews and Gentiles, this message is Christ, who
> is the power of God and the wisdom of God (1 Cor
> 1:23-24).

Paul will boast in nothing except the cross of Christ.
He understands that the cross is the wisdom of God
and the power of God. He also knows that it is only
through dying with Christ that we can live with him:

> I have been put to death with Christ on his cross,
> so that it is no longer I who live, but it is Christ
> who lives in me. This life that I live now, I live by
> faith in the Son of God, who loved me and gave his
> life for me (Gal 2:19-20).

When we die to ourselves, die to sin in ourselves, die to
ourselves by accepting suffering in our lives, we find
our true selves. Each of us can then say, "It is Christ
who lives in me." St. Peter has a word of great comfort
for people who have physical suffering to bear in life:

> Think of what Christ suffered in this life, and then
> arm yourselves with the same resolution that he
> had: anyone who in this life has bodily suffering has
> broken with sin, because for the rest of his life on
> earth he is not ruled by human passions but only by
> the will of God (1 Pt 4:1-2, *Jerusalem Bible*).

Suffering, then, is not an unmitigated disaster to
be avoided at all costs. Suffering with Christ is a great
blessing and brings with it a new freedom from sin.
The Christ who suffered and died for us comes to live
in us in a new way when we are prepared to suffer and
die with him.

It is knowledge of the Lord which transforms suffering from a curse to a blessing. As Paul said, "All I
want is to know Christ." From this knowledge of

Christ, this living, personal, intimate union with Christ, comes the experience of the crucified Jesus. Jesus is not dead. He is risen. And the sufferings which he underwent on the way to his glorious resurrection are now called his *blessed* passion.

We should mention that *in Christ* we have the strength to share in his sufferings; apart from Christ we have no strength. Christ has taken on himself the sufferings of the whole world. As Isaiah foretold:

> "But he endured the suffering that should have
>   been ours,
>   the pain that we should have borne.
> All this while we thought that his suffering
>   was punishment sent by God.
> But because of our sins he was wounded,
>   beaten because of the evil we did.
> We are healed by the punishment he suffered,
>   made whole by the blows he received" (Is 53:4-5).

The sufferings of Christ have brought us peace and healing. It is Christ who bears our sufferings. We do not bear the sufferings of others. No matter how deeply moved we may be by the sufferings of a loved one, we should never ask the Lord to allow us to bear that suffering. It is Christ alone who can bear our suffering. It is by his wounds alone that we are healed.

Healing and Suffering

Healing and suffering are not mutually exclusive. A gospel of healing which excludes the spiritual value of suffering is not the gospel of Christ. Similarly, a gospel of redemptive suffering which excludes divine healing is not the gospel of Christ. Speaking in a general way we can say that in the past, the emphasis was placed too exclusively on the redemptive value of suffering without specific reference to the healing power of the Spirit through prayer and the sacraments.

Today, in the usual pendulum swing, the emphasis, especially in some literature, is on the healing efficacy of prayer and the sacraments, almost to the total exclusion of the redemptive nature of suffering. We must constantly keep restoring the balance.

American priest George Kosicki of the Bethany House of Intercession gets the balance right in a letter to a suffering friend. He writes: "Healing is a step toward the cross in that healing removes the obstacles to freely embracing the cross." And in a word of Christian wisdom he says to those with sufferings in their lives: "Don't waste them! They are too precious. By sufferings that are sanctified we enter into the eternal sacrifice for the salvation of souls. This is our part in the cross. The Lord seeks such worshippers in Spirit and in truth."

Pope John Paul II brings the same message to the suffering throughout the world. He invites them and urges them to offer up their sufferings in union with the crucified Lord for the whole church.

Suffering in union with Christ becomes a powerful prayer of intercession. Jesus invites each of us to take up our cross and follow him. There is no easy way of being crucified with Christ! We cannot decide which cross we are going to carry this day. The cross in our life today is that factor, rarely of our own choosing, through which we can die to ourselves, to our own self-will and self-seeking, to our inordinate passion for pleasure, comfort and ease. It may be the hostility of someone we have to work with, or it may be the loss of a very dear friend; it may be a headache or a paralysis; it may be the loss of our reputation or the failure of our work. Whatever it is, we must either accept it or reject it. If we accept it in union with Christ, the suffering involved is transformed and we carry our cross in union with Christ.

The suffering which we accept in union with Christ is not simply for our own purification but for the salvation of the whole world. When we suffer with Christ we intercede with the Father for all humanity. There is, then, no contradiction between "offering up" all our pains, sorrows and sicknesses in union with Christ for our own spiritual growth and the salvation of the world, and, at the same time, pleading with God for mercy and healing. In fact, to joyfully embrace the cross which Christ wishes us to carry, we very often need deep healing. We need to be healed, in the first place, of the spiritual blindness which prevents us from seeing that it was necessary for the Messiah to suffer, and we need to be healed too of our lack of faith and trust in God and his infinite mercy. To joyfully embrace the cross we need to be healed of the deep-rooted selfishness which makes us reluctant to accept suffering of any kind and prevents us from rejoicing in the cross of Christ. St. Paul shows us the way:

> I have learned this secret, so that anywhere, at any time, I am content, whether I am full or hungry, whether I have too much or too little. I have the strength to face all conditions by the power that Christ gives me (Phil 4:12-13).

To those who suffer Jesus always says:

> "Come to me, all of you who are tired from carrying heavy loads, and I will give you rest. Take my yoke and put it on you, and learn from me, because I am gentle and humble in spirit; and you will find rest. For the yoke I will give you is easy, and the load I will put on you is light" (Mt 11:28-30).

When we pray with those who are suffering we are

responding to this invitation. We are bringing the suffering brother or sister to the Lord so that the Lord can give his rest. The rest which the Lord gives may take the form of a physical or an emotional healing, when the person is entirely freed from pain and sickness, or it may be a deeper rest in the spirit, when, through a new acceptance of God's will, the person becomes more closely united with the crucified Christ. We do not determine the type of rest which the Lord gives. We are only ministers, servants of our sick brothers and sisters, bringing them to the Lord so that the Lord can bless them.

As we pray with the sick and the suffering, we announce to them the good news of God's healing love. But we should also speak to them about the real value of suffering offered to God. Nothing is more disheartening to a sick person than a visit from one who believes neither in divine healing nor in the redemptive value of suffering. The Christian always brings to the sick a message of hope—hope for the sick person through divine healing, and hope for the salvation of the world through redemptive suffering in union with Christ.

We will give St. Paul the last word on suffering:

> But to keep me from being puffed up with pride because of the many wonderful things I saw, I was given a painful physical ailment, which acts as Satan's messenger to beat me and keep me from being proud. Three times I prayed to the Lord about this and asked him to take it away. But his answer was: "My grace is all you need, for my power is greatest when you are weak." I am most happy, then, to be proud of my weaknesses, in order to feel the protection of Christ's power over me. I am content with weaknesses, insults, hardships, persecutions, and difficulties for Christ's sake. For when I am weak, then I am strong (2 Cor 12:7-10).

THREE:
Healing in the Church

St. Luke wrote his two-volume work, the gospel and the Acts of the Apostles, to show that what God began in the power of the Spirit through the ministry of Jesus, he continues through that same Spirit in the name of Jesus in the ministry of the church. All ministry is in the name of Jesus and in the ministry of the church. All ministry is in the name of Jesus and in the power of the Spirit.

The 72 disciples whom Jesus sent out to preach the good news discovered the power of his name:

> The seventy-two men came back in great joy.
> "Lord," they said, "even the demons obeyed us
> when we gave them a command in your name!" (Lk 10:17).

The name of Jesus is so powerful because when we speak or act in his name he himself is present. The name *Jesus* is like no other name. St. Paul says:

> . . . God raised him to the highest place above
>   and gave him the name that is greater than any
>   other name.
> And so, in honor of the name of Jesus
>   all beings in heaven, on earth, and in the world
>   below
>   will fall on their knees,
> and all will openly proclaim that Jesus Christ is
>   Lord,
>   to the glory of God the Father (Phil 2:9-11).

33

To carry on his ministry in the world Jesus has given us the gift of the Holy Spirit and the gift of his own name. He authorizes each of us to act in his name. What we do in his name is done by him. He specifically promises:

"The Father will give you whatever you ask of him in my name" (Jn 15:16).

Asking in the name of Jesus, speaking in the name of Jesus, acting in the name of Jesus—that is what we mean by Christian ministry.

We see St. Peter exemplifying this ministry:

"I have no money at all, but I give you what I have: in the name of Jesus Christ of Nazareth I order you to get up and walk." (Acts 3:6).

Peter said, "I give you what I have." What did he have? He had the authority to speak in the name of Jesus. This miracle of healing the cripple who sat by the gate of the Temple had such an impact that many of the people of Jerusalem turned to the Lord. The chief priests and leaders were so alarmed that they asked one another:

"What shall we do with these men? Everyone in Jerusalem knows that this extraordinary miracle has been performed by them, and we cannot deny it. But to keep this matter from spreading any further among the people, let us warn these men never again to speak to anyone in the name of Jesus" (Acts 4:16-17).

Notice that the chief priests did not forbid them to speak about Jesus. They forbade them to speak in the name of Jesus. They knew the difference between speaking about a person and speaking in the name of the person. To speak about a person implies that the person is absent; to speak in the name of the person makes the person present. And that is what the chief priests feared most of all—the presence of Jesus. Wherever a disciple was speaking in the name of Jesus, Jesus himself was present. And so we have that very specific prohibition mentioned in Acts:

> So they called them back in and told them that under no condition were they to speak or teach in the name of Jesus (Acts 4:18).

Instead of frightening the disciples, this prohibition only emphasized the source of their strength, the name of Jesus, and so the whole community of believers began to pray for an ever greater manifestation of the power in the name of Jesus. This is the first recorded prayer of the church in Jerusalem:

> "And now, Lord, take note of their threats and help your servants to proclaim your message with all boldness, by stretching out your hand to heal and to work miracles and marvels through the name of your holy servant Jesus" (Acts 4:29-30, *Jerusalem Bible*).

The disciples had been warned not to preach in the name of Jesus. In this prayer they prayed for boldness and courage in the face of this threat. They will get boldness and courage to proclaim the gospel when God stretches out his hand to heal. It is what God does in the name of Jesus that fills them with courage. The disciples did not pray just for courage to face the threats of the chief priests. Courage is not just an inner ability to overcome fear. Courage is aroused in the disciples when they see what God is doing. So, the first followers of Jesus prayed for miracles in the face of persecution. That was their answer to the chief priests. They had been forbidden to preach in the name of Jesus; now they prayed for even greater miracles in the name of Jesus. And God answered their prayer.

> As they prayed, the house where they were assembled rocked; they were all filled with the Holy Spirit and began to proclaim the word of God boldly (Acts 4:31).

In the face of persecution the church prayed for miracles of healing in the name of Jesus and God answered that prayer. The church was not afraid to ask God to intervene in dramatic ways. The disciples were asking that the people see the power of the name of Jesus. We should surely make that prayer our own. The church today faces many threats and difficulties. We will have the courage and boldness to face them when God stretches out his hand to heal and work miracles in the name of Jesus.

The Acts of the Apostles is the story of the church in the first century, the story of what the Lord was doing in his disciples. Wherever the disciples went they brought the good news of Christ, and they brought God's healing love to his people.

> As a result of what the apostles were doing, sick people were carried out into the streets and placed on beds and mats so that at least Peter's shadow might fall on some of them as he passed by. And crowds of people came in from the towns around Jerusalem, bringing those who were sick or who had evil spirits in them; and they were all healed (Acts 5:15-16).

As a result, we are told,

> More and more people were added to the group—a crowd of men and women who believed in the Lord (Acts 5:14).

Jesus himself had given as proof of his teaching the

works that he performed through the Holy Spirit. He now enables his disciples to offer the same proof. The proof of the gospel is not found in eloquent words but in deeds performed by the power of God's Spirit. Mark makes this point very clearly:

> The disciples went and preached everywhere, and the Lord worked with them and proved that their preaching was true by the miracles that were performed (Mk 16:20).

Here we see the continuity between the ministry of Jesus and the ministry of the disciples. It is the Lord Jesus who is working with the disciples, and the Lord is proving their message not through irresistible logic or philosophy but by miracles. What we do in the name of Jesus is the proof of what we teach or preach. St. Paul was very convinced of this truth. He wrote to the troublemakers in Corinth:

> If the Lord is willing, however, I will come to you soon, and then I will find out for myself the power which these proud people have, and not just what they say. For the Kingdom of God is not a matter of words but of power" (1 Cor 4: 19-20).

For the establishment of the kingdom Christ has given us the very same power that he himself received from the Holy Spirit. It is that power which we must use. And if we are not using that power the church of Christ will not grow. There is no other power capable of building the kingdom. And all that power is given in the name of Jesus. We see how St. Paul understood his ministry:

> In union with Christ Jesus, then, I can be proud of my service for God. I will be bold and speak only about what Christ has done through me to lead the

Gentiles to obey God. He has done this by means of
words and deeds, by the power of miracles and
wonders, and by the power of the Spirit of God
(Rom 15:17-19).

In the early church the disciples did exactly the same
works as Jesus himself did. They preached the gospel,
healed the sick, and cast out demons. And these works
were the sign that their preaching was true.

The Church's Faith in Healing Today

We have considered how the early church not only believed in divine healing but prayed for God to
work miracles of healing. What does the church
believe about divine healing today? The simplest and
most direct way to answer this question is to examine
how the church prays for healing in her prayers,
especially in the liturgy. The principle is this: If the
church prays for something in the liturgy, she believes
that her request is according to the mind of God, and
that God will grant the request. Liturgical prayers,
therefore, are an immediate source for studying the
faith of the church. Pope Pius XII in his great encyclical
letter, *Mediator Dei*, said:

> The entire liturgy has the Catholic faith for its con-
> tent, inasmuch as it bears public witness to the faith
> of the Church. For this reason whenever there was
> a question of defining a truth revealed by God, the
> Sovereign Pontiff and the Councils in their recourse
> to the theological sources, as they are called, have
> not seldom drawn many an argument from this
> sacred science of the Liturgy. For an example in
> point, our predecessor of immortal memory, Pius IX
> so argued when he proclaimed the Immaculate Con-
> ception of the Virgin Mary. Similarly during the
> discussion of a doubtful or controversial truth, the

Church and the Holy Father have not failed to look
to the age-old and time honored sacred rites for
enlightenment. Hence the well-known and venerable
maxim *"legem credendi, lex statuit supplicandi"*—the
rule of life indicates the rule of faith (Nos. 47-48).

In his well-known *Allocution to the Assisi Congress of
Pastoral Liturgy* in 1956 Pius XII said:

It would be very difficult to find one truth of the
Christian faith which is not expressed in some way
in the liturgy. In the liturgy the Church com-
municates abundantly the treasures of the deposit of
faith, of the truth of Christ.

To find out what the church believes, we must study
her prayers. This study is open to all the faithful.
Anyone who can pray the prayers of the church can
ask, What does the church mean in this prayer? This
will be our approach in the rest of this book. We will
look at the prayers of the liturgy, the prayers which the
church says in her sacraments, and we will ask
ourselves the question, What is the church really asking for in this prayer or in this sacrament?

In *The Constitution on the Sacred Liturgy*, the Second Vatican Council tells us:

The liturgy is the outstanding means by which the
faithful can express in their lives, and manifest to
others, the mystery of Christ and the real nature of
the true Church (No. 2).

The prayers of the liturgy manifest our faith in God. In
our prayers we ask God for strength in our weakness,
healing in our sickness, forgiveness in our sinfulness,
joy in our sorrows, light in our darkness. We pray to be
filled with the Spirit, to be filled with the power of his
gifts. These prayers reveal our God. Our God is a God
who saves, who heals and delivers from evil, who com-

forts, enlightens and strengthens his people. That is
the God we worship, and those are the blessings we ask
from our God. If, in the sacred moment of liturgical
worship, the church prays to the Father in the name of
Jesus for health of mind and body, for deliverance from
evil, and for joy in sorrows, we know that request is in
accordance with God's will. We know that the church,
because she makes this request, believes in divine healing. The answer to the question, Does the church
believe in divine healing?, must be an emphatic yes,
and the reason we give is this: throughout her liturgical
worship the church keeps praying for health of mind
and body.

FOUR

The Sacrament of Reconciliation

According to the revised rites of the liturgy, the sacrament of reconciliation is to be called a sacrament of healing. In the introduction to the new rite of this sacrament we read:

> In order that this sacrament of healing may truly achieve its purpose among Christ's faithful, it must take root in their entire life and move them to more fervent service of God and neighbor (No. 7).

We have always understood that this sacrament was a great sacrament of forgiveness. Sin, especially mortal sin, had to be brought to this sacrament. And with the forgiveness of sin was an experience of peace. But why does the new rite call this sacrament a sacrament of healing? What is healed? The answer to these questions is also given in the introduction to the rite:

> Just as the wounds of sin are varied and multiple in the life of individuals and of the community, so too the healing which penance provides is varied (No. 7).

The Wound of Sin

The wound of sin is a new concept in Catholic consciousness. We have seen sin as an offense against God, and through the sacrament of penance we have

41

always sought pardon for that offense. Now the church speaks about the wounds of sin and presents the sacrament of penance as a sacrament of healing, bringing varied healing for the multiple wounds of sin. We must become familiar with this new concept.

Sin is an offense against God, but it also inflicts a wound not only on the sinner, but on his or her neighbor, and indeed on the whole church. Parents sin by neglecting their children, but they also wound their children by this neglect. Children sin by abandoning their parents and not showing them gratitude and love, but they also wound their parents by such a lack of love. For the sin itself there is divine forgiveness; for the wound of sin there is divine healing.

The wound of sin is an inner wound. The person is wounded in his or her self-esteem, self-image, relationships or memory. We will be considering how all these different wounds are healed—inner healing—in the sacrament of reconciliation.

As a working definition of "inner healing" we can accept the following: Inner healing is an experience of the healing love of God in which the person realizes that he or she is lovable (healing of the self-image), or capable of loving and forgiving someone (healing of relationships), or able to gratefully accept some past event (healing of memories). We will see, in a practical way, how all these healings come through the celebration of the sacrament.

For the multiple wounds of sin there is a manifold gift of healing in the sacrament of reconciliation. Confessors must become more sensitive to the presence of the wound of sin and more aware of the fact that in this sacrament they are not just ministers of God's pardon but also ministers of God's peace. Pardon is for the sin; peace is for the inner healing. In the prayer of absolution the priest exercises both ministries. He prays, "Through the ministry of the church may God give you pardon and peace."

Self-image

Very often the individual sins in a person's life are the direct result of a wound of sin in the person's self-image. Self-image is the way we feel and think about ourselves. It underlies all the stances we take in life, and it permeates all our attitudes to life. Sometimes a person may have all the outward signs of success and competence yet feel totally inadequate. The reason is a poor self-image. This wounded self-image can be the cause of many individual sinful actions. For instance, some people who are "born liars" might simply love to tell lies. On the other hand, perhaps they are so wounded in their self-image that they feel a compulsive need to present themselves in a better light. And so they always try to make themselves out to be better or more successful than they really are. The confessor may give beautiful moral exhortations on the need to speak the truth, but only prayer for the inner healing of the self-image will set them free. A person who can accept himself or herself as lovable will no longer feel the need to lie.

Discernment

The most important rubric in the new rite of the sacrament of reconciliation is this:

> Priest and penitents should prepare themselves above all by prayer to celebrate the sacrament. The priest should call upon the Holy Spirit so that he may receive enlightenment and charity (No. 15).

Without this prayer of the priest and penitent, and

without the enlightenment of the Holy Spirit, the confessor will not be able to discern the deeper needs of the penitent. The new rite states that the penitent must "be cured of the sickness from which he suffered" (No. 6). It is only through the light of the Holy Spirit that the confessor can discern the nature of the sickness. The confessor who has not discerned the wound of sin may exhort the penitent and encourage the person to do his or her best in the future, whereas the confessor who has discerned the wound of sin will pray with the penitent for inner healing. Speaking of confessors the new rite says:

> In order that he may fulfill his ministry properly and faithfully, understand the disorders of souls and apply the appropriate remedies to them, and act as a wise judge, the confessor must acquire the needed knowledge and prudence by constant study under the guidance of the Church's magisterium and especially by praying fervently to God. For the discernment of spirits is indeed a deep knowledge of God's working in the human heart, a gift of the Spirit, and an effect of charity (No. 10).

We must pray for the gift of discernment. And we must also learn to listen to the word of God. That is why the new rite encourages priest and penitent to listen together to a short reading of scripture. The sacrament is a celebration of the word of God, the word which announces peace and forgiveness, and the word which gives light. The new rite states:

> Through the word of God Christians receive light to recognize their sins and are called to conversion and to confidence in God's mercy (No. 17).

A celebration of the word of God, when confessor and

penitent listen together to the word, should be an integral part of each sacramental confession. God's word is our light. To understand ourselves, to gain insight into our inner selves and the wounds of sin within we need that light. We must rely on the word of God. As scripture says:

> The word of God is alive and active, sharper than any double-edged sword. It cuts all the way through, to where soul and spirit meet, to where joints and marrow come together. It judges the desires and thoughts of man's heart. There is nothing that can be hid from God; everything in all creation is exposed and lies open before his eyes. And it is to him that we must all give an account of ourselves (Heb 4:12-13).

The word of God proclaimed in the celebration of this sacrament lights up the inner darkness and in this new light both priest and penitent begin to see the way forward. Since we have the light of the word of God we should never celebrate this sacrament in darkness!

When we are dealing with the wounds of sin it is often very helpful to listen to a word of scripture which speaks of gratitude and praise. For instance the following verse of the psalm can be very helpful:

> Praise the Lord, my soul!
> All my being, praise his holy name!
> Praise the Lord, my soul,
> and do not forget how kind he is (Ps 103:1-2).

As confessor and penitent respond to this invitation and praise God with their whole being, the wounds of sin will quickly show up because the person will find it difficult if not impossible to praise in the area where he or she is wounded.

An example will illustrate this. As I was praying

with a woman who had a deep sadness within her I began to praise God for her whole life, especially for her father. At this point she broke down. She was illegitimate and never knew her father. She couldn't praise God because of the deep anger and self-hatred within. The cause of the self-hatred was the wound in her self-image. She was ashamed of her parents and she blamed her father. I now knew the area where the inner healing was needed, that is, in her relationship with her father. But first of all she had to be led in a prayer of repentance. She was not accepting God's providence in her life. In fact, deep down she was in utter rebellion against God for allowing her to be born of such a union. There could be no healing without repentance. The new rite states:

> We can only approach the Kingdom of Christ by *metanoia*. This is a profound change of the whole person by which we begin to consider, judge, and arrange our life according to the holiness and love of God, made manifest in his Son in the last days and given to us in abundance. The genuineness of penance depends on this heartfelt contrition. For conversion should affect a person from within toward a progressively deeper enlightenment and an ever-closer likeness to Christ (No. 6).

This person did not "consider, judge and arrange her life according to the holiness and love of God." Instead, she was seeing herself and her parents through the eyes of this world. Instead of judging according to God's love, she was judging according to the hypocritical standards of this world. Why should she, a mature adult, live with a deep sense of shame and disgrace? Why was she in such a deep rebellion against God's plan in her life?

We prayed through three stages. First we asked God's pardon for not accepting his divine providence in our life. This prayer was not too difficult. We prayed:

> Father, we ask you to pardon all the many and secret ways in which we rebel against your providence in our lives. We ask your pardon for that deep pride in our hearts which always seeks to impose our plan and refuses to acknowledge your divine plan in our lives.

She had confessed many sins in her past life, but she had never acknowledged this sin of rebellion against God's providence. She had never recognized it as a sin. In fact, the more she rejected God's plan in her birth the more virtuous she thought she was! The more we allow ourselves to be dominated by the world's notion of virtue and respectability the blinder we become to real sin. Real sin is always rooted in that pride which refuses to submit to God. God's ways are not our ways. This woman was unconsciously demanding that God's way must always be her way. This is the first stage of conversion for the proud spirit, the stage of humble submission to God and the acceptance of his plan in our life.

The second stage of this prayer was one of thanksgiving. We thanked God for his providence in our lives. I led her in this prayer:

> Father, I thank you for your divine providence in my birth. Father, it was you who knit me together in my mother's womb. I thank you for the wonder of my being.

She found this prayer much more difficult to say, but as we persevered in thanking God, she began to feel with the prayer. (It is always necessary to stay with the hard prayer of thanksgiving until the person begins to feel with the prayer. In this way the person either comes into the real prayer of thanksgiving or a new obstruction to the prayer of thanksgiving is revealed. This is a most important means of discernment.)

When she felt reasonably comfortable with this prayer of thanksgiving I then led her in a prayer of praise and thanks for her father:

> Father, I bless and thank you for her father wherever he may be at this moment, and I ask you to fill him with your Spirit. I bless you that you chose him to be her father.

At first she could not even listen to this prayer. Then she felt she would be hypocritical even to repeat the words because she felt no gratitude in her heart for that man. I then asked her to ask Jesus to say the words for her and to fill her with such forgiveness for her father that she would really be grateful to God for him. She now could see Jesus praising God for her father, and as we persevered with this prayer she began to experience the new heart which God promises:

> I will give you a new heart and a new mind. I will take away your stubborn heart of stone and give you an obedient heart. I will put my spirit in you (Ez 36:26-27).

She became grateful for her father and began to experience a great love for him. As we continued to praise God, she was freed from all shame and resentment. She began to experience the meaning of the words of absolution: "Through the ministry of the Church may God give you pardon and peace." She began to experience a deep peace. For the first time she began to be grateful to God for the gift of her life. The world had told her she was a bastard, and she had lived by that word. Now God was free to tell her that she was his beloved child and that her father, no matter what his mistakes (and Jesus told us never to judge), was chosen and blessed by God. As her relationship with her father was healed—as she forgave her father—she experienced a deep healing in her own self-image. She knew who she was. And she was grateful. She was now able to enter more deeply into the prayer of the Mass: "In mercy and love unite all your children wherever they may be." She was now including her father in this prayer. Previously, while she was rejecting her father and not acknowledging him in any way before God, she was unconsciously excluding him from the Eucharist. She wanted to be brought together in unity with everyone except him! And so the Eucharist could not be an experience of deep unity within the body of Christ. Now that her primary relationship with her father had been healed, she began to experience, through her daily Mass, deep healing in many other relationships in her life.

If I had not led her through those three phases of repenting her sin against God's providence, of praising God for his providence, and of praising God for her father, who was at the center of her self-rejection, she would not have experienced that inner healing in the sacrament. Her conversion would not have been complete.

The new rite states:

> Penance always entails reconciliation with our brothers and sisters who remain harmed by our sins (No. 5).

There is no inner emotional wound of sin which will not be healed through the sacrament of reconciliation. We have, in this sacrament, God's healing for the whole church. But the penitent must be led, by the light of the Spirit and by the gift of discernment, to recognize the nature of the wound. Without praying together and pondering the word of God together, as the rubrics of the sacrament require, the confessor and the penitent will have no light. There will be no discernment and very little inner healing.

The Confessor's Role

Speaking of the confessor's role of leading the penitent into a deeper conversion of heart, the new rite says:

> By receiving repentant sinners and leading them to the light of the truth, the confessor fulfills a paternal function: he reveals the heart of the Father and shows the image of Christ the Good Shepherd. He should keep in mind that he has been entrusted with the ministry of Christ, who mercifully accomplished the saving work of human redemption by mercy and by his power is present in the sacrament (No. 10).

The confessor has to reveal "the heart of the Father and show the image of Christ the Good Shepherd." He does this by the way in which he receives penitents, the way in which he prays with them for the light of the Holy Spirit and the gift of discernment, the way in which he listens to the word of God and, finally, by the way in which he allows the Spirit to lead him as he prays for the inner healing which the penitents need. As penitents approach the confessor, no matter how burdened they may be, they should experience a total acceptance—an acceptance which is not just a sign of the confessor's good will, but an acceptance which is a clear sign of the Father's loving embrace, an incarnational sign of the presence of the Good Shepherd.

Some penitents are burdened with sins which fill them with shame and great spiritual distress. To help such sufferers one penitent has written her testimony.

God set her completely free from the sinful habit of masturbation which she always found difficult to mention. This woman, whom we will call Jane, writes:

> I bless the day I met you and you led me to confess my sins against my own body. I had a strong habit of masturbation which bothered me for many years. I had confessed my sin on various occasions in the anonymity of the confessional, but I had never really faced the problem. It isn't easy to confess sins of a sexual nature, and it is not easy to break a long established habit. I am convinced that conversion can only come through being open to the Holy Spirit. Your talks helped me and encouraged me to allow the Holy Spirit into the weakest area of my life.
>
> Your ministry in the sacrament of reconciliation was so gentle and yet so direct that I felt the presence of the Holy Spirit working through you. You prayed over me and I felt a great weight being lifted off me and a tremendous feeling of joy welling up within me. I knew I had been set free. What I could not achieve by my own efforts and good resolutions over the years had happened instantaneously by the power of the Holy Spirit made effective through your prayer. I will celebrate forever the joy of that moment.

Two points stand out in Jane's testimony. First, we need to allow the Holy Spirit into the weakest areas of our lives. (We usually invite him into the areas which we think are not too bad!) Second, we need gentle but direct ministry. Since masturbation is sometimes a sign that the person is rejecting his or her sexuality, I encouraged Jane to invite the Holy Spirit into the whole area of her sexuality and ask him to help her accept herself as a woman. I then encouraged her to recognize that masturbation is sinful, and that the Holy Spirit has been sent among us for the forgiveness of sins. As she became aware of the Holy Spirit entering the sinfulness in her sexual being, she was set free and her whole sexual being was healed.

God's answer to sinfulness is always forgiveness in the Spirit; the human answer to sinfulness is all too often a rationalization of the sinful habit, the sin is explained away. Confessors or counsellors, recognizing that people may be under such compulsive habits that they are no longer free and wanting to ease the burden of guilt, occasionally tell penitents not to worry, that sin cannot be committed in such a state. Such advice leads to depression and not to liberation. It takes the whole problem out of the Lord's hands and deprives penitents of their only hope of freedom, the healing forgiveness of Jesus in the sacrament of reconciliation.

When we humbly acknowledge something as sinful, then we have the infinite power of our Savior to free us. Instead of saying, "Don't worry, this cannot be sinful," the confessor or counsellor should say, "Have great hope because since you acknowledge this as sinful Jesus will set you free." And then confessor and penitent should pray for that freedom. As Jane wrote in her testimony, "You prayed over me and I felt a great weight being lifted off me and a tremendous feeling of joy welling up within me." Before I discovered the power of ministering through prayer I also tried to relieve people's burdens by rationalizations. Now I know that Jesus does not want us to rationalize away the sinful habits which burden people, but to free them from those habits through healing prayer.

The sacrament of reconciliation has been given to us by Christ for the healing of the whole person. But without confession, without the grateful acknowledgment in the presence of God of our need for forgiveness, there can be no healing. St. John says,

> If we say that we have no sin, we deceive ourselves,
> and there is no truth in us. But if we confess our
> sins to God, he will keep his promise and do what is
> right: he will forgive us our sins and purify us from
> all our wrongdoing (Jn 1:8-9)

To be human is to be a sinner. Our sinfulness will
always express itself in our actions. Sinful actions are
manifestations of a sinful heart, but they are also signs
of a wounded heart. It is most important to bring the
wound in the heart, not just the sin, to the sacrament.
The following letter from a religious sister whom we
will call Rose illustrates how the wound of sin is healed
and how this is often accompanied by physical healing.
Sister Rose writes:

> This is a small testimony I want to share with you.
> For 10 years I have suffered from osteoarthritis and
> rheumatoid arthritis in my feet, ankles and spine,
> and also from decalcifying of my bones which made
> it very painful for me to kneel for any length of
> time.
> The first week I was here Father Jim was ad-
> dressing us, and I got the urge to speak to him
> about myself. So I made an appointment and Father
> saw me that afternoon, when he prayed with me for
> some time. Toward the end of the session I felt a
> great calm and peace which I had not experienced
> for some years. As the day went by I began to feel
> less pain and stiffness, and before the month was
> over my arthritis was completely gone and has never
> returned. With our Lady I can say, "The Lord has
> done great things for me."

The significant phrase in Sister Rose's testimony is
this: "I got the urge to speak to him about myself." A
good confession, a confident and joyful laying of one's
whole life before God in the person of the confessor,

opens up the whole person to a new experience of God's healing love. In Sister's case, the hurts, the resentments and the anger of a whole life surfaced in prayer and as these deep wounds were healed in the sacrament she began to experience physical healing as well.

Sister Rose had been hurt badly in her life. Even in her childhood she had been very unhappy because of a bad relationship with her mother. When she entered the convent she was hurt again. These hurts were the cause of the uncharitable thoughts and feelings which plagued her. Because of these uncharitable thoughts she felt that she was living a sinful life, unable to forgive and forget. In fact, she was living a heroic life of charity, fighting every day against those thoughts which were the pain in her inner wound. As the inner wound healed, especially through her daily union in the Eucharist with all those who had hurt her, the real sign of forgiveness, she was no longer troubled with those thoughts and began to experience a complete physical healing of many ailments. All this healing began through a good confession.

When people read this kind of story they often say, "But I have never had that kind of experience in confession!" The sad truth is that the new rite of reconciliation has not truly been implemented yet. We have changed the external formulas and rites; we have, in some places, even moved from the confessional box to a reconciliation room. Yet if we are not faithful to the spirit of the new rite, the celebration of the sacrament will be greatly impoverished, and people will not receive the blessings that the Lord has for them. To celebrate the sacrament without sharing the word of God is a violation not only of the external rite but, much more seriously, a violation of the whole spirit of the new rite. The word of God provides the light which both penitent and confessor need. It is the word of God which announces God's healing; it is the word of God which brings the promise of God's pardon. Yet many people, perhaps the majority, still confess their sins without hearing the life-giving word of God.

In my own experience as a confessor I have to say that when there was no celebration of the word of God, when there was no time spent in prayer with the penitent, when people were only interested in a "quick absolution," I never witnessed any healing. This has led me to the strong conviction that absolution is not enough. Absolution is essential to the celebration, but if the celebration is reduced to the absolution we have a deformation of the sacrament. The time factor is irrelevant. The fact that others may be waiting should not influence the confessor in the way he exercises the healing ministry of Christ in this sacrament. Better a few well-celebrated confessions than many hurriedly made confessions! To give life to this sacrament, to make this sacrament an experience of the healing love of Christ, priest and penitent must be prepared to give time—time for prayer together, time for listening to the word of God together, and time to give thanks to God together. Penitents who are only seeking absolution from their sins will receive pardon, even if their confession only lasts a minute. But such penitents will not experience healing.

In the new rite of the sacrament of reconciliation we have a most powerful means for the healing and the spiritual renewal of the whole person. This is God's gift to his church in our day. We should make good use of it.

FIVE:
The Sacrament of the Sick

In the letter of St. James we read,

Is anyone among you in trouble? He should pray. Is anyone happy? He should sing praises. Is there anyone who is sick? He should send for the church elders, who will pray for him and rub olive oil on him in the name of the Lord. This prayer made in faith will heal the sick person; the Lord will restore him to health, and the sins he has committed will be forgiven. So then, confess your sins to one another and pray for one another, so that you will be healed (Jas 5:13-16).

The church, throughout the ages, has faithfully acted on this word of scripture. The church's liturgical ministry to the sick takes the form of the sacrament of anointing. Unfortunately this sacrament, which we used to call extreme unction, became associated with death rather than with healing. Thus when the priest was called to a sick person it was a sign of the gravity of the situation rather than a sign of hope or recovery. But, even in the days when this sacrament was only given to those in grave danger of death, the Christian community had some evidence of the healing power of Christ at work. Indeed the Council of Trent stated that physical healing sometimes takes place through this sacrament:

57

The thing signified is the grace of the Holy Spirit whose anointing takes away sins if there be any still to be expiated, and also the remains of sin, and raises up and strengthens the soul of the sick person by exciting in him great confidence in the divine mercy, supported by which the sick one bears more lightly the miseries and pains of his illness and resists more easily the temptations of the devil who lies in wait for his heel; and at times, when expedient for the welfare of the soul, restores bodily health.

Even though the church taught in her official doctrine that bodily health is sometimes restored through anointing, however, the expectation of healing was most often lacking in the sick person, in the family, and even in the priest. The sacrament was seen most often as the "last rites"—the immediate preparation for death. And certainly priests and others throughout the centuries have commented on the great peace and tranquility anointing brought to dying persons.

The New Rite

In the new rite of anointing the sacrament is called the sacrament of the sick, and it is seen in terms of Christ's ministry to the whole person. In the introduction to the new rite we read:

The Lord himself showed great concern for the bodily and spiritual welfare of the sick and commanded his followers to do likewise. This is clear from the gospels, and above all from the existence of the sacrament of anointing, which he instituted and which is made known in the Letter of James (No. 5).

It is the Lord's concern which is manifested in this sacrament. Through the celebration of the sacrament the sick person encounters our Lord himself and experiences his saving and healing presence. That is why the sick person should never delay the sacrament; for such an encounter with the Lord he or she should be as alert as possible. This is how the new rite describes the effects of this sacrament:

> This sacrament gives the grace of the Holy Spirit to those who are sick: by this grace the whole person is helped and saved, sustained by trust in God, and strengthened against the temptations of the Evil One and against anxiety over death. Thus the sick person is able not only to bear suffering bravely, but also to fight against it. A return to physical health may follow the reception of this sacrament if it will be beneficial to the sick person's salvation. If necessary, the sacrament also provides the sick person with the forgiveness of sins and the completion of Christian penance (No. 6).

Emphasis is clearly on "the grace of the Holy Spirit" by which "the whole person is helped and saved." The whole person is not just the physical being. Therefore, this healing through the grace of the Holy Spirit should not be seen only in terms of physical cure but of relationship with God, the source of all being. Healing means wholeness, and wholeness is the effect of spiritual well-being, not just physical well-being. Father Paul Hynes, O.P, a writer who has had experience of considerable sickness, offers the following distinction:

> Healing, for our purpose, has to be distinguished from curing. In the first case the person is delivered from the burden of his suffering but the physical or mental disability may remain. It is no longer a source of anxiety nor does it alienate the person from others, or even from God as the case may be. In the case of a cure all signs of illness disappear.

Nearly all medical treatment aims at a cure, although it may involve the removal of a diseased organ leaving an obvious scar. If this or similar treatment is not possible very little effort is made to heal the person, in our sense of the word, and this is probably the biggest criticism that can be made of the general medical service in the West.[1]

There are incurable diseases, but there is no incurable person. That is why we can pray with absolute faith for the healing of the person. The healing of the person must always be seen as the healing of the heart; the healing of the person in his or her relationship with God and with other people; the freeing of the person from deeply buried resentments, fears and non-acceptance of God's plan in his or her life. Yet with equal faith we must also pray for the physical healing the person needs. The very prayers we say require such a faith of us. As we anoint the sick person we say:

> Through this holy anointing
> may the Lord in his love and mercy help you
> with the grace of the Holy Spirit. . . .
> May the Lord who frees you from sin
> save you and raise you up (No. 124).

> Lord Jesus Christ, our Redeemer,
> by the grace of your Holy Spirit
> cure the weakness of your servant N.

> Heal his/her sickness and forgive his/her sins;
> expel all afflictions of mind and body;
> mercifully restore him/her to full health,
> and enable him/her to resume his/her former
>   duties,
> for you are Lord for ever and ever (No. 125).

[1] Paul Hynes, O.P., "The Church's Ministry for the Sick," *Doctrine and Life*, Nov. 1982, p. 551.

In this sacrament we pray repeatedly for health of mind and body. And since the church teaches that restoration of physical health is one of the effects of this sacrament, we should earnestly request it in our prayer. If the sick person is at the point of death, we are directed in the rite to pray for the Lord to sustain him or her:

> Lord Jesus Christ,
> you chose to share our human nature,
> to redeem all people, and to heal the sick.
>
> Look with compassion upon your servants,
> whom we have anointed in your name with this
> holy oil
> for the healing of their body and spirit.
>
> Support them with your power,
> comfort them with your protection,
> and give them the strength to fight against evil.
> Since you have given them a share in your own
> passion,
> help them to find hope in suffering,
> for you are Lord for ever and ever (No. 77).

The liturgy of the sacrament is all-important. It should be celebrated with great solemnity and with the fullest participation of the sick person's family, friends and parish. It is a celebration of the word of God which calls the sick person and his or her friends to a renewed faith. The priest should always seek to arouse this faith by a few words of encouragement. Having listened to the word of God I find that a short reflection on how the word of God is fulfilled in the sacrament evokes a new faith in the sick person. The word is fulfilled because the sacrament brings the grace of the Holy Spirit by which the whole person is brought to health. The sick person must be encouraged to open his or her whole life to this grace. The priest should encourage the sick person to offer his or her whole being and all cares and worries to the Lord. The prayer of St. Ignatius is very inspiring:

> Take, Lord, and receive all my liberty,
> my memory, my understanding, and my entire will,
> all that I have and possess.
> You have given all to me.
> To you, O Lord, I return it.
> All is yours,
> dispose of it wholly according to your will.
> Give me your love and your grace,
> for this is sufficient for me.

We should never take faith for granted. Our constant prayer has to be, "Lord I believe, help my unbelief." The community of faith, gathered around the sick person, must seek to arouse by its own faith a new expectation. The Lord is present in the celebration. In his presence we must make a complete offering of ourselves. The sick person must be encouraged to offer everything to the Lord who is present. When the sacrament is celebrated in this faith, when the sick person is led to make a complete offering to God, a profound healing of the whole person takes place. It is not only the sick person who receives this healing; the family will be healed also. Sickness is a time of crisis. When serious sickness befalls a member of a family, the whole family is affected and needs to be called to greater faith and commitment. As the family members surrender the sick person, with confidence, into the loving providence of God, they receive a great blessing through the celebration of this sacrament. The priest should always pay special attention to the family so that the sickness which threatens one member will become the occasion of a new experience of trust and confidence in God for all. As Francis Groot writes:

A renewal of the pastoral care of the sick is badly
needed in our modern, secularized society. Modern
man seems unable to face sickness and death, which
have become taboos. The sick and the aged are ac-
commodated outside society, in hospitals and special
homes. In such a situation it is up to the Christian
community to show to the sick that they are still
wanted and needed; and wanted as they are, old,
sick and disabled, for it is thus that they contribute
to the well-being of the Church through their
association with the passion of Christ. The regular
visitation by members of the Christian community—priests, deacons, faithful—offer the afflicted
consolation and hope. Such regular visitation will
culminate in the celebration of the sacrament of
healing anointment, not because the patient is get-
ting worse, but as a sign of hopeful acceptance of a
God-given situation.[2]

It is especially during the time of sickness that the
world should be able to see how Christians love one
another and how they can face sickness and death
strong in faith.

The healing of the whole person which the sacrament of anointing imparts is sometimes accompanied
by physical healing. The following letter from a Poor
Clare sister describes such a physical healing:

In 1969, due to acute back pain, the specialist
ordered an X-ray and it showed that a disc between
two of the lumbar vertebrae was abnormally thin.
This meant that when certain actions were performed, the bones rubbed together and caused pain.
I was fitted with a surgical corset and had to wear it
day and night. In 1971, after a fall, I was taken to
the hospital and put in traction for 14 days and

[2] F. Groot, "The Sacrament of the Sick," *Doctrine and Life*, Aug. 1977, p.
39.

fitted with another corset. Then, on Friday, June 24, 1977, during our annual retreat, I received the sacrament of the sick after being prayed over for the release of the Spirit and physical healing. A few days after the retreat, when life was back to normal, I realized that my back pain was not so severe. When the days turned to weeks the pain just went, so I took the steel strips out of the corset, and then after another few weeks I left the corset off altogether and now it is collecting dust and taking up room in our cupboard! It is also a reminder to thank God for his wonderful healing power through his sacrament of the sick and also an occasion to pray for all his priests who administer his sacraments.

When I first mentioned healing to that sister she said that she was happy to carry her cross and that she was "offering up" her bad back. I was very impressed by her spirit. I then asked her, "How can you be so sure that this is God's will?" Somewhat taken aback she said, "Well, I will pray about it today." The next day she asked for prayer for healing.

This sister was the youngest member of a rather elderly enclosed community. As we celebrated the sacrament of anointing, the whole community gathered around her and laid hands on her and prayed the prayer of faith for her healing. God heard that prayer, and her back was healed. Now she is the abbess of that community. I say to her when we meet, "God had to give you a good strong back before he laid that burden on your shoulders!" Had we not prayed for healing her back would not have been healed. Furthermore, had her whole community of sisters not prayed with her as we celebrated the sacrament I am convinced that the healing would not have taken place.

This experience convinced me that we should always seek to have the sick person surrounded by a believing community as we celebrate this sacrament. On this occasion all the circumstances fostered faith. These Poor Clare Sisters were a fervent community and they had just completed their eight-day retreat. During the retreat I had spoken a lot about God's healing love in the sacraments, and they believed. The sister in question was most open to the Lord and willing to do his will in all things. She would have been happy to suffer for the rest of her life because in her suffering she found union with Christ crucified. In the deep faith of that community we were able to pray the prayer of faith in the sacrament and ask confidently for her healing.

Pain

In her prayer for the sick the church always asks God to free the sick from affliction. Some years ago I went to see a woman who was sick with the shingles and in great pain. Four of her friends were there, and we formed a community of faith and prayer around her. Then we celebrated the sacrament of the sick. As soon as she was anointed all the pain left her and she got up. She never had another moment of pain. I was so struck by this immediate relief from pain that I went back to study the prayers of the rite. There, in the blessing of the oil, I found the answer:

> May your blessing +
> come upon all who are anointed with this oil,
> that they may be freed from pain and illness
> and made well again in body, mind and soul.

The very first request in the blessing was for the sick person to be freed from pain. This, I believe, is sufficient reason to anoint people who have acute pain. If the oil is blessed for the relief of physical suffering—as well as mental and spiritual affliction—it should be used for that purpose. Of course, those in pain must prepare themselves to celebrate a sacrament and receive the Holy Spirit. The oil is not magic! As mentioned above, those preparing to receive the anointing must confess their sins and open their whole life to the Holy Spirit. They have to surrender their whole being to God. They must be led to pray with St. Ignatius, "Take, Lord, and receive all my liberty, my memory, my understanding, and my entire will, all that I have and possess."

The woman with the shingles was completely open to God. She later told me that when she realized that the Lord had healed her she knelt down in her room and prayed, "Lord, you have healed my body, now heal my soul." And she received a most special grace of union with Christ our Lord. The physical healing was only the preparation for this grace of union with Christ.

Depression

The sacrament of the sick is very often what people suffering from tension, depression or anxiety most need. A very depressed priest once asked for prayer for healing. Another priest and myself prayed with him. We formed around him a community of faith and then we celebrated the sacrament of the sick. Sometime later he wrote:

> I feel a different person. Before you blessed me I was and had been deep down in depression and riddled with tension. Today I want to shout alleluia and thank God for his goodness and mercy. I am actually looking forward to flying back to my mission in Africa. A few weeks ago I never thought it possible. Praised be Jesus Christ.

This priest had been home sick for a whole year, and even though he was attending a nursing home run by religious he had never been anointed. He was receiving all the medical care possible, he was receiving great love and support, but he had not received the one thing necessary for health of mind and body: the sacrament of the sick.

Ever since this experience I always encourage depressed people to prepare themselves for this great sacrament. And the Lord always blesses them. Surely, when we come before the Lord and open our whole being to him and invite the Holy Spirit to enter into our lives, God cannot refuse to bless us. That is what we do in receiving this sacrament. Not every depressed person has received the same total healing as this priest. But I have noticed that whenever a small community of faith gathers to support the depressed person, even two people, the sick person always receives great relief.

Loss of Confidence

A priest who had spent most of his life in academic work was appointed to a parish. As soon as he arrived in the parish he lost all confidence in himself. He was unable to say public Mass or preach. A friend brought him for prayer. We formed a small community of faith around him and prayed for him. As I anointed him, we were able to pray in faith the prayer of the rite, "Grant him full health, so that he may be restored to your service." The next Sunday he said the public Masses. The Lord restored his confidence, fulfilling the promise he made through Isaiah:

> "I am the high and holy God, who lives forever. I live in a high and holy place, but I also live with people who are humble and repentant, so that I can restore their confidence and hope" (Is 57:15).

When faced with a suffering person, whether the anguish is in body, mind or spirit, we can always bring great comfort through healing prayer and especially through the sacrament of the sick. The gravity of the sickness cannot be measured simply in physical terms. The mental anguish which drives a person to suicide may not in itself appear a serious illness. How sick is the person who has lost complete confidence in himself? How sick is the person suffering from agoraphobia? What about the person whose crippling sense of guilt persists despite the ministry of the confessor in the sacrament of reconciliation? In all these cases I offer the sufferer the consolation of the sacrament of the sick, and the fact that the Lord heals them from agoraphobia, guilt, fear, pain, loss of confidence, depression and tension convinces me that this is the right thing to do.

The minister of Christ is a physician of souls. He can never be satisfied until he sees a change in the person. If the sacrament of reconciliation does not bring healing for the inner wound of sin, the priest must continue his investigations. His ministry has not been effective and he should not put the blame on the penitent, much less on the Lord! What new ministry does the penitent need? Using the gift of discernment, for which he should always pray, the priest allows the Holy Spirit to guide him. Sometimes, I have discovered that the inner healing, which I normally associate with the sacrament of reconciliation, comes through the sacrament of anointing. At other times the Spirit leads the priest to discern the need to set the person free through a prayer of deliverance. The priest must be convinced that as the physician of the soul the Lord gives him both the discernment and the power needed to bring the person into the peace of Christ. There is no technique. If he does not know what to do next to help the person he must simply ask the Lord and wait. The Lord will always show him the next step. There is always something more he can do. He can wait, and listen, and pray, and give the Lord the chance to direct him.

An example will illustrate the need for listening:

> Agnes couldn't stay alone at night after her mother died. She had nursed her mother for many years and was most devoted to her. If her husband was not at home, she would have to go to a neighbor's house and wait for him. Her sister and I prayed with her. I was convinced that a simple prayer was all that was needed. But the fear persisted. Because of her weakened and nervous state I decided to anoint her. But the fear remained, and I knew that our ministry to her was not complete. As we waited I prayed, "Lord, what do I do now?" I got a sense that the right thing to do would be to bless the house. I asked if she had ever had the house blessed, and she said no. So I blessed water and salt and the three of us went through the house blessing it. As soon as the blessing was finished all the fear left her and never returned.

When the simple prayer with Agnes didn't free her from fear, I knew that there was something more needed. When the sacrament of anointing didn't get rid of the fear, I knew with even greater certainty that something else was needed. It was then that the Lord directed me to bless the house. This experience has taught me to be very pragmatic in my ministry. If one thing doesn't work, try something else! But allow the Lord to direct each step.

Priests sometimes say to me: "I do not have that kind of time to give to people." Regrettably this is true.

Many priests haven't got the time to exercise fully the ministry for which they were ordained and anointed by the Spirit because of all the other tasks they have to do. And, for these other tasks, they have received no anointing from the Lord! Speaking to the French bishops, Pope John Paul II said:

> It is most important for priests to be freed to devote themselves fully to the ministries that are proper to them and are their particular responsibility, as dispensers of the mysteries of God and as spiritual guides.[3]

There is surely something seriously wrong if the complexities of parochial administration deprive the priest of the time he needs for prayerful and discerning celebration of the sacrament of anointing. Since the priest is ordained to celebrate the sacraments for God's people, the quality of that celebration, the prayerful and discerning time given to that celebration, and the involvement of the people, the penitent or the sick person and his or her friends in the celebration, must be his primary concern. No other parochial task, no matter how important it may be in itself, should ever infringe on the time which the priest needs to perform his sacramental ministry. What Dr. Vance Havner said about the preacher is equally true of the celebrant of the sacraments:

> I think preachers are getting lost in a multitude of smaller duties. The preacher has a peculiar place in the economy of God. He is in danger of becoming so involved in secondary affairs that he loses his prophetic gift. The devil doesn't care how great a success a preacher is in any field, if he can just kill the prophet in him.[4]

---

[3] *L'Osservatore Romano*, Nov. 15, 1982, p. 9.
[4] See D. Coggan, *On Preaching* (London, 1978), p. 14.

If people in need cannot find in the celebration of the sacraments the peace which Christ came to bring, where will they find it? A top priority in the church today is not just more priests, but more time for priests to exercise their priestly ministry. And as priests begin to give more and more time to the celebration of the sacraments and their prophetic role of preaching and teaching, who will do all the other things in the parish which have to be done? As we look at the renewal of the sacraments in the life of the parish through the liberation of the priest from all his non-priestly functions, we see the immediate need for the emergence of all the lay ministries within the church.

SIX:
The Holy Eucharist

The Second Vatican Council reminded us that the Eucharist is at the very center of our worship of God and our life as the people of God:

> The other sacraments, as well as every ministry of the Church and every work of the apostolate, are linked with the holy Eucharist and are directed toward it. For the most blessed Eucharist contains the Church's entire spiritual wealth, that is, Christ Himself, our Passover and living bread. Through His very flesh, made vital and vitalizing by the Holy Spirit, He offers life to men. They are thereby invited and led to offer themselves, their labors, and all created things together with Him.
>
> Hence the Eucharist shows itself to be the source and the apex of the whole work of preaching the gospel (*Decree on the Ministry and Life of Priests,* No. 5).

We know, with the instinct of faith, that the Mass is the most important act of worship in our life. In the Mass perfect worship is offered to God our Father, because in the Mass it is Jesus Christ, our High Priest, who is offering himself to the Father.

Speaking of the institution of this great sacrament the Council said:

At the Last Supper, on the night when He was betrayed, our Savior instituted the Eucharistic Sacrifice of His Body and Blood. He did this in order to perpetuate the sacrifice of the Cross throughout the centuries until He should come again, and so to entrust to His beloved spouse, the Church, a memorial of His death and resurrection: a sacrament of love, a sign of unity, a bond of charity, a paschal banquet in which Christ is consumed, the mind is filled with grace, and a pledge of future glory is given to us (*Constitution on the Sacred Liturgy,* No. 47).

The Mass is the eternal sacrifice of Christ made present to us sacramentally under the species of bread and wine. The priest, as he extends his hands over the bread and wine, prays:

Let your Spirit come upon these gifts to make them holy so that they may become for us the Body and Blood of Jesus Christ your Son.

Just as it was through the power of the Holy Spirit that Jesus was conceived and became man in Mary's womb, so it is through the power of the same Spirit that the bread and wine are transformed into the Body and Blood of Christ.

The Presence of God

As we celebrate the Mass we enter into the presence of God. To prepare ourselves to enter into God's holy presence we acknowledge our sinfulness and we pray not just for pardon but also for healing. The very consciousness of our sinfulness and our wounds makes us conscious of the healing power of Christ and we pray,

> You were sent to heal the contrite, Lord have
> mercy.

Aware of the division caused by our sins we confidently confess our sins and we pray,

> Lord Jesus, you heal the wounds of sin and division,
> Christ have mercy.

While the church seeks to make us aware of our sinfulness right at the beginning of the Mass, she also makes us aware of God's healing love. Throughout the Mass we grow in our awareness of our sinfulness, but we also experience a corresponding growth in our awareness of God's healing love, culminating in the great act of faith before communion when we cry out,

> Lord, I am not worthy to receive you, but only say
> the word and I shall be healed.

I—my whole person, my whole being, in body, mind and spirit—I shall be healed.

In the Mass, as we become conscious of our need for forgiveness we hear the comforting words,

> This blood will be shed for you and for all men so
> that sins may be forgiven.

With great confidence we pray,

> Lord Jesus Christ . . .
> Look not on our sins but on the faith of your
>   Church.

And, with expectation in our hearts we cry out three times:

> Lamb of God, you take away the sins of the world:
> have mercy on us.

Still mindful of our sinfulness and our need for forgiveness the priest prays,

Lord Jesus Christ, Son of the Living God, by the will of the Father and the work of the Holy Spirit your death brought life to the world. By your holy body and blood free me from all my sins and from every evil. Keep me faithful to your teaching and never let me be parted from you.

Having acknowledged our sinfulness many times throughout the Mass and asked God's forgiveness, we are now ready to receive holy communion. Once again we are reminded that we have been saved from our sins. The priest proclaims:

This is the Lamb of God
who takes away the sins of the world.
Happy are those who are called to his supper.

To which we reply with a final and confident confession and petition,

Lord, I am not worthy to receive you,
but only say the word and I shall be healed.

The Mass, which begins with the confession of sins, reaches its climax in the confident prayer for healing: "But only say the word and I shall be healed." We used to pray, "But only say the word and *my soul* shall be healed." This was a misleading phrase. Sometimes people got the impression that the church prayed only for the soul and not for the body. And so this phrase has been changed. The emphasis now is clearly on the whole person: "I shall be healed."

Prayers for Healing in the Eucharist

The church always prayed for the healing of the whole person just before communion. An alternative to the prayer used in the private preparation of the priest given above is:

> Lord Jesus Christ, with faith in your love and mercy I eat your body and drink your blood. Let it not bring me condemnation but health of mind and body.

As he purifies the sacred vessels the priest prays,

> Lord, may I receive these gifts in purity of heart. May they bring me healing and strength now and for ever.

What are these prayers for health of mind and body asking for? Our expectations must correspond to our words. If the sentiments in our hearts are not in accord with the words on our lips, we are not really praying at all.

Just after the Lord's Prayer in the Mass, when we have acknowledged God as our Father, we pray:

> Deliver us, Lord, from every evil,
> and grant us peace in our day.
> In your mercy keep us free from sin
> and protect us from all anxiety.

Notice how the church prays very specifically for protection from all anxiety. Jesus forbade us to be anxious or fretful, and yet we can so easily give in to crippling anxiety. A psychiatrist once commented that about 90 percent of his patients were mentally sick because of anxiety, and that anxiety is a spiritual condition which he can do very little to alleviate. The answer to anxiety is trust in God. And so, in the Mass, in the prayer for a threefold deliverance, we pray to be protected from anxiety. The prayer, of course, does not work magically. We have to obey the word of God. We must surrender all our anxieties and worries.

It is, of course, quite possible to pray, "protect us from all anxiety," while in our hearts we harbor worries and fears. If we hold on to our worries, we cannot be protected from them by God. God never forces our freedom. He invites us to allow him to take care of all our fears, anxieties and worries. He assures us in scripture that he is our rock, our protection, our stronghold, our deliverer. But he awaits our free cooperation. Just as Jesus had to say to the man by the pool, "Do you want to get well?" so he says to us, "Do you want to be protected from your anxieties? Do you want to never worry again?" If we do, then the Lord will most certainly protect us from anxiety.

To appreciate how intensely the church prays for healing throughout the year it is good to examine the post-communion prayers of the Mass. These are beautiful prayers, too often ignored because they are the last prayers of the Mass. The post-communion prayer generally consists of two parts. In the first part we thank God for the grace of this holy Eucharist which we have just celebrated, and in the second part we ask that this Eucharist will effect some very specific help in our life. For example,

> Lord,
> may our sharing in this mystery
> free us from our sins
> and make us worthy of your healing (*Friday after Ash Wednesday*).

> Lord, through this sacrament
> may we rejoice in your healing power
> and experience your love in mind and body (*Monday of the First Week of Lent*).

The request in the second prayer is very daring. We pray for "an experience of God's saving love in mind and body." It is one thing to have a theoretical knowledge that God's love is a healing love. It is quite another thing to experience God's love as healing. In the Mass the church does not hesitate to ask for this experience. We, too, should pray that we may rejoice in God's healing power. We all believe in God's healing power; we can only rejoice in it when we experience it. That is why the church prays, to "experience your saving love in mind and body." To say this prayer with faith we must open our whole being to God and allow the healing love of God to fill us. We open our minds and submit to the all-holy God and allow the presence of God's healing Spirit to renew and transform our minds. We surrender all care and worry, all fear and doubt, and we invite God to renew us.

Consider another post-communion prayer:

> Lord our God, renew us by these mysteries. May they heal us now and bring us to eternal salvation (*Thursday of the First Week of Lent*).

Notice the word "now" in that prayer. The church wants something to happen *now*—not tomorrow or the next day, but now! It is now, in this hour, that we need to know the healing presence of God. A final prayer of the Good Friday liturgy makes this point well:

> Almighty and eternal God,
> you have restored us to life
> by the triumphant death and resurrection of Christ.
> *Continue this healing work* within us.
> May we who participate in this mystery
> never cease to serve you.

All these prayers for healing within the Mass indicate how strongly the church believes in God's healing love, and how she expects that healing power to be experienced in the Mass. Does our faith correspond to the faith of the church? Do we believe as strongly in divine healing? With so many prayers for the healing of body, mind and spirit in the Mass, isn't it extraordinary that so many of us have either ignored these prayers or not allowed them to form our faith? Many of us, I fear, do not really expect divine healing. We expect forgiveness of sins, but we do not expect the healing of the wounds of sins.

The Glory of God

We pray for healing in the Mass, but we do not offer the Mass for healing. We offer the Mass, in the first instance, for the glory of God. It is God who is at the center of the Mass, and it is God's right to glory and not our need for healing which is uppermost in the mind of the church. And yet, God's right to glory and our need for healing come together in a most marvelous way because God is glorified in us, in our openness to his Spirit, in our growth in his own image and likeness. God is glorified when we are healed. The Eucharist, offered for the glory of God, heals within us everything that is opposed to that glory. In the Eucharist we have healing for all resentment, bitterness, anger, selfishness and lack of forgiveness. But to receive that healing we must do as the Lord commands:

> "If you are about to offer your gift to God at the altar and there you remember that your brother has something against you, leave your gift there in front of the altar, go at once and make peace with your brother, and then come back and offer your gift to God" (Mt 5:23-24).

If we do not seek reconciliation with our brother or sister, God will not be glorified in our celebration, and there will be no healing. Notice that Jesus does not say, "If you remember that you have something against your brother. . . ." He says, "If you remember that your brother has something against you." He doesn't ask if your brother is justified or not! Too often we say, "I have nothing against him," and proceed to blame him for having something against us! Participation in the Eucharist requires unconditional forgiveness for each person in our life. Conditional forgiveness is not Christian—we are not to meet the other person half way, we are to go all the way! Forgiveness withheld impedes the healing power of the Eucharist. Notice that in the penitential rite we prayed, "You were sent to heal the contrite." Jesus does not heal those who are not contrite.

The Vatican Council was very aware of the need for forgiveness for a fruitful celebration of the liturgy.

> Before men can come to the liturgy they must be called to faith and conversion (*Constitution on the Sacred Liturgy*, No. 9).

The homily seeks to instill this spirit of conversion. In the homily the priest takes the word of God and applies it to our particular situation. In each situation conversion is the prerequisite for full participation. Without ongoing conversion there can be no deepening of faith in the Eucharist. And without a deep faith there will be no healing.

Many times during the Mass we cry out, "Lord have mercy." We throw ourselves on the mercy of God. To receive God's mercy we must be prepared to share it with everyone. If there is one person in our life with whom we are not fully sharing the mercy of God, one person to whom we do not offer unconditional forgiveness, we need conversion. Without this conversion our sins will not be forgiven and we will not experience the healing love of God:

> You cannot expect the Lord to pardon you while you are holding a grudge against someone else. You yourself are a sinner, and if you won't forgive

another person, you have no right to pray that the
Lord will forgive your sins. If you cannot get rid of
your anger, you have no hope of forgiveness (Sir
28:3-5).

The Sign of Peace

Seen in the context of forgiveness asked for and
forgiveness shared, the sign of peace is one of the most
significant gestures of the whole Mass. The priest
prays:

> Lord Jesus Christ, you said to your apostles:
> I leave you peace, my peace I give you.
> Look not on our sins, but on the faith of your
>   Church,
> and grant us the peace and the unity of your
>   kingdom
> where you live for ever and ever.

He then wishes the whole community peace:

> The peace of the Lord be with you always.

The peace of the Lord is not just for each individual to
keep. It is for sharing with all. And so we are invited to
share that peace:

> Let us offer each other the sign of peace.

The sign of peace signifies our readiness and will-
ingness to be at peace with everyone. If there is one
person excluded, the sign loses all its meaning and the
word of Jesus challenges us:

> "If you love only the people who love you, why
> should you receive a blessing? Even sinners love
> those who love them! And if you do good only to
> those who do good to you, why should you receive
> a blessing? Even sinners do that! And if you lend
> only to those from whom you hope to get it back,

why should you receive a blessing? Even sinners lend to sinners, to get back the same amount! No! Love your enemies and do good to them; lend and expect nothing back. You will then have a great reward, and you will be sons of the Most High God. For he is good to the ungrateful and the wicked. Be merciful just as your Father is merciful" (Lk 6:32-36).

The sign of peace indicates our desire to be in union and harmony with all our brothers and sisters. It is a sign of readiness to forgive unconditionally. Without this unconditional forgiveness we cannot share the Eucharist. Peter asked Jesus about this type of forgiveness:

"Lord, if my brother keeps on sinning against me, how many times do I have to forgive him? Seven times?

"No, not seven times," answered Jesus, "but seventy times seven" (Mt 18:21-22).

The sign of peace must be given, not just to the person next to us, but to the whole community. We say to the whole community, "Now that I have asked and received forgiveness from the Lord, I am offering to each one of you forgiveness and peace." If we are not sincerely offering peace to all, we cannot receive peace ourselves, and if we are not receiving peace from the Lord, all our inner wounds remain unhealed. It is possible to go to Mass with a raging resentment against someone, and return home after Mass with the raging resentment. The Mass is not magic. If we do not forgive, we are not forgiven. Since it is through forgiving us that God heals us, if we make it impossible for God to forgive, by our own unforgiveness, we at the same time make it impossible for God to heal. God cannot heal the unforgiving heart. This means that we can celebrate the Eucharist, even every day, but if we are not prepared to forgive "seventy times seven" we will never experience the inner healing which the Eucharist contains.

The following testimony illustrates how one person experienced the healing power of God in the Eucharist:

> Five years ago I was praying for my husband whose addiction to gambling was causing more than just financial problems. However, one day at Mass I found myself instead asking God if he thought the time was right for me to have a baby. If he thought so it would be OK with me, but he'd have to look after me! My problems were quite bad enough as they were.
>
> Peace has reigned ever since that day. I have a caring, supportive and hardworking husband who is the proud father of a delightful 4-year-old son.

During the Mass she received the grace to entrust herself and her whole future to God, and she was set free from the feelings and worries she had been caught up in. She was able to pray "protect us from all anxieties" with new conviction because now she was willing to surrender all her anxieties to the Lord.

SEVEN:
A Service of Prayer for Healing

All healing comes through the word of God. The word of God should not just be heard, it should be celebrated. The healing service provides an opportunity for both proclamation and celebration. The service itself is paraliturgical, similar in many ways to the penitential service which the church recommends today. A typical service consists of two parts. Part I includes scripture readings, prayers and hymns (see the example which follows). Part II offers the prayers for healing and an anointing with blessed oil.

Theme: THE NEW COVENANT

God Promises the New Covenant: Jeremiah 31:31-34
   Proclaiming of the text.
   Listening in silence and receiving the promise in our hearts.
   Responding through spontaneous praise and thanks.
   Responding in song.

God Proclaims the New Covenant: Luke 22:14-20
   Proclaiming of the text.
   Listening with grateful heart.

Penitential reflection: "This cup is God's new covenant sealed with my blood, which is poured out for you."
Responding in praise and thanks.

Paul Announces That the New Covenant Consists in the Holy Spirit: 2 Corinthians 3:4-6

Proclaiming of the text.
Listening prayerfully to the text.
Becoming aware in silence of the presence of the Holy Spirit.
Responding to the presence of the Spirit in prayers of thanks to the Father and to Jesus.
Responding in song.

The Spirit Helps Us in Our Weakness: Romans 8:26

Proclamation of the text.
Listening prayerfully to the text.
Becoming aware of the area of our greatest weakness.
Inviting the Spirit to enter into this area of weakness.
Praising the Spirit for being the strength in our weakness, the light in our darkness, the holiness in our sinfulness.
Responding in song.

This concludes the first part of the service and normally takes about 30 minutes. It provides the opportunity for a deep listening to the word of God. The steps in the prayer are fourfold: hearing the promise of God proclaimed in the word, welcoming the promise with gratitude, accepting that the promise is being fulfilled, and beginning to act on the promise. After each short scripture reading there is time for silent, prayerful listening, followed by spontaneous prayer of praise and thanksgiving. In a large congregation it is best if the celebrant leads this spontaneous prayer and then invites the whole community to respond in a hymn of praise.

In the second part of the service the celebrant prays for healing in different areas of life. I normally pray for healing in these four areas: memories, relationships, spiritual healing, and physical healing. We will consider each separately.

Healing of Memories

Prayer for healing should consist mainly in prayer of praise and thanks. C.S. Lewis once said, "Praise is inner health made audible." Praise, then, is a very appropriate prayer to use in praying for inner healing. In praying for the healing of memories we are asking God for a grateful memory. Our memory, through which we can recall everything that has ever happened to us, should be patterned on the Eucharist. The Eucharist is the grateful memory of the church, calling to mind the passion and death of Jesus and giving God praise and glory. We should be able to call to mind our whole life and give God praise and glory for it. This means that we should be able to praise God for our sorrows, failures, disappointments and frustrations, just as we praise him for our joys and successes. The inability to praise God for some past event is a sign of a wound in the memory. As we become aware through prayer that we are wounded, we acknowledge the wound and we ask Jesus to come and heal it, to heal the memory. We ask Jesus to make us grateful. People who have been hurt are often advised to forget about it. That suppresses the memory, and it will only lead to future disturbance. The suppressed memory, like an underground river, must break forth somewhere. People, even in old age, can be troubled by childhood memories which they have suppressed. Suppressed childhood memories can undermine self-confidence. Even a person who has attained eminent professional success can be undermined by childhood memories which rise up and attack in unguarded moments.

Allen Wheelis, a widely-known psychiatrist and writer, recounts a childhood memory revolving around his father, who died when Wheelis was a young boy:

> My father and I have never parted. He made his mark on me that summer, and after his death that fall continued to speak on a high-fidelity system within my conscience, speaks to me still, tells me that I have been summoned, that I am standing once again before him on that glass porch giving an account of myself, that I will be found wanting, still after all these years a "low down no-account scoundrel," and that his judgment will be binding on my view, that I shall not now or ever be permitted to regard myself as innocent or worthy.
>
> These things, accepted as true, make one a slave, have made me and make me still, fifty years after those pale blue eyes have gone to the grave. Whenever a current situation calls upon me to stand forth, to present myself, my father speaks again with undiminished authority. His denunciation yields guilt and anxiety, tends to drive me out of human society into the wilderness alone, thereby to confirm ever more deeply the image of myself as unworthy to live with others, having nothing to say, deserving of no recognition.[1]

This is how Wheelis describes the physical symptoms which accompany the inner denunciation which comes from his father:

> Steel fingers seize my heart. My chest constricts as if

[1] Allen Wheelis, *How People Change* (New York: Harper & Row, 1974).

in a giant hand, I struggle to breathe, to continue talking. My sentences break down . . . I hang up the phone which is dripping wet in my clenched fist.[2]

This great man was a victim of a suppressed childhood memory, which he explores in great detail in the book. He needed healing. And only Jesus can reach back and heal the memory.

Praising God for some past event is the clearest sign of accepting God's providence. The story of a woman we will call Alice illustrates how the Lord heals the memory.

Alice experienced tension and sadness in her life for many years. A tragic event had occurred when she was only 11 years old. Her father was dying of cancer, and the drugs which the doctor was prescribing to ease the pain were not very effective. When the pain got very bad her father would call Alice and dictate a very abusive letter to the doctor. Eventually the little girl refused to write any more abusive letters for him. Finally, her father said to her, "If you don't write this letter, I will do something you will regret for the rest of your life." At that, Alice ran out of his room and went to stay with another member of the family. Two days later her father committed suicide. Her mother and brothers and sisters helped her greatly at the time, but now, 40 years later, she felt deep anguish of spirit.

When we had discerned that the cause of Alice's deep sadness and tension was the memory of refusing to write the letter, I invited her to join me in praising God. We praised God specifically for the fact that she didn't write that letter. Unconsciously she had been saying to herself all these years, "If only I had written that letter, I would not have been the cause of my

[2] Ibid.

father's death!" All through the years she had carried this great burden of guilt. As she began to praise God—and it was very hard for her to do so initially—the burden lifted and she was set free and came into a new joy and freedom in the Holy Spirit.

So often the cause of sadness in a person's life is an unhealed memory—a hidden resentment, a suppressed guilt, an unconfessed and forgotten sin. (Forgotten sins will always surface because time cannot take away sin, only Jesus can do so.) As we begin to praise God for our whole life, for every single thing that has ever happened, these unhealed memories surface. We become aware of them through our inability to praise God for them.

Praising God in the face of adversity is, of course, a very biblical response.

> I know what it is to be in need and what it is to have more than enough. I have learned this secret, so that anywhere, at any time, I am content, whether I am full or hungry, whether I have too much or too little. I have the strength to face all conditions by the power that Christ gives me (Phil 4:12-13).

Prayer for the healing of memories provided a marvelous opportunity for encouraging people to cast all their cares on the Lord and to trust him in everything. It is important to begin this prayer by asking God's pardon:

> Father, we thank you for the great gift of memory. We thank you that through memory we can recall all your many blessings. We ask your pardon for the way in which we abuse memory, for the way in which we make our memory a storehouse for resentment, bitterness, grievances, unforgiveness and self-pity.

Lord Jesus, we ask you to come and touch each memory and make it truly grateful. We praise you for every moment of joy and success, and we bless you too for every moment of sorrow and failure. We praise you, Father, for every moment of sadness, disappointment and frustration.

As we allow the Spirit to guide us in these prayers of thanks for the whole of life, we begin to experience a marvelous presence of God. The celebrant leads this prayer, and the congregation enters into the prayer in silence. As people begin to praise God in the silence of their heart for their whole past life, and as they ask Jesus to make them truly grateful to the Father and to heal their memories, tremendous inner healing takes place. Using the words of the Psalm 103 we pray:

Praise the LORD, my soul!
All my being, praise his holy name! (Ps 103:1).

We use the following principle as our guide:
Anything within us which refuses to bless the holy name of God needs healing (or conversion).
All that is within us is registered in our memories. Therefore, when we call upon all that is within us to bless God, we are bringing our whole being, our whole experience of life, good and bad, into a new relationship with him.

Normally I take about 10 minutes on this prayer. I explain the nature of the wound in the memory, speak about grateful memories and how the Mass is the grateful memory of the church, drawing attention to the nature of the prayer of praise as the complete acceptance of God's divine providence in life and, finally, allow the main areas of life to be prayed for—parents, childhood, adolescence, adulthood, and so forth. Invariably there is the same response in all congregations: a deep prayerful silence in which people have an experience of the liberating hand of the Lord setting them free from bitter memories.

There is no memory, no matter how deep and no matter how bitter, which the Lord will not heal. As Christians we should never say to a person troubled with a bad memory, "Try and forget it!" Rather we should say, "Let us praise God for this memory and ask Jesus to heal it."

Healing of Relationships

Bitter memories are often the root cause of bad relationships. Having prayed for the healing of memories, we now pray for the healing of relationships. Again, we center our prayer in the Eucharist. In the Mass we pray for unity and peace:

> May all of us who share in the body and blood of Christ
> be brought together in unity by the Holy Spirit
> (*Eucharistic Prayer II*).

And we share that love, peace and forgiveness through the sign of peace.

In the healing service we ask the Lord to heal within us everything which prevents us from loving as he does. We ask him to set us free from our arrogance and pride, from criticism and backbiting, and from all unforgiveness. We do not judge the person with whom we have a bad relationship; we take responsibility for the relationship and ask the Lord to heal the source of our inability to love and forgive. We pray:

> Father, I bless you for so many brothers and sisters with whom I have the privilege of sharing my life. I ask your pardon for all the many ways in which my own selfishness prevents me from sharing.

Lord Jesus, I ask you to come and heal within me everything which prevents me from loving as you love, from forgiving as you forgive. Remove my merciless and hard heart, and fill me with the mercy and compassion of the Father so that I can share your love with everyone.

Having asked the Lord for this forgiveness, we now share it. The celebrant leads the congregation in a prayer of reaching out to the people in their lives and offering the unconditional forgiveness of Christ to each one. He prays:

Lord Jesus, we go out now in the power of your Spirit, and we forgive each person in our life.

Since the deep hurts of life can only be caused by those who are nearest and dearest to us, it is always necessary to forgive them. Allen Wheelis, mentioned above, will have to forgive his father who, with the best of intentions and thinking only of his son's future, marked him for life. Wheelis will never be free until he forgives his father and praises God for him. It is necessary to forgive parents, children, husband or wife, schoolteachers, close friends, in the name and power of Jesus. Great healing takes place within families when the husband says, "Lord, I forgive my wife," and the wife says, "Lord, I forgive my husband"; when parents say, "Lord, we forgive our children," and children say, "Lord, we forgive our parents." As the congregation prays these prayers, the Lord is present healing and restoring his people. We not only forgive, but we ask the Lord to bless those we have forgiven, to bless them and fill them with his Spirit.

This prayer of forgiveness transcends time and place. We can reach out beyond the grave and forgive someone who has died. This realization is, in itself, an occasion of great joy for many people. Death is no obstacle to the Spirit of the Lord. So, in the Lord's Spirit, we can bless and forgive the dead. Through this prayer the congregation begins to understand in a new way the meaning of the communion of saints. As people are led through this prayer to forgive the dead, perhaps a dead spouse or parent, they experience great release and spiritual joy. The celebrant leads the prayer and the congregation responds in the silence of the heart. But in those silent hearts the Spirit is performing a wonderful work of healing and re-creation: "Behold, I make all things new."

Spiritual Healing

Spiritual healing is liberation from all destructive habits of sin and from every bondage of the devil. In the Mass we proclaim,

> Lord, by your cross and resurrection
> you have set us free.
> You are the Savior of the world.

Yet many people do not experience freedom in their lives. They experience bondage. They live bound to destructive habits of sin and very often they despair of ever being set free. In the Mass we pray,

> Deliver us, Lord, from every evil,
> and grant us peace in our day.

Yet even when a person is praying for freedom, evil sometimes seems to triumph. That great prayer for deliverance in the Mass must be applied to the area of the person's bondage—drugs, alcohol, sexual abuses, the occult, and so forth. We have the assurance of Jesus, "If the Son sets you free, then you will be really free."

Jesus sets us free from all the bondage of the evil

one, and he gives us the authority to set others free in his name. The prayer for spiritual healing takes the form of a command in the name of Jesus. It is a prayer to be said with reverence and calm.

> Lord Jesus, we rejoice in your victory over Satan and sin, and we rejoice that you share your victory with us. Lord, in your name and with your authority, I bind every evil spirit.

When we bind Satan in the name of Jesus, he cannot resist. He is bound. The celebrant now pronounces freedom in the name of Jesus:

> In the name of Jesus I cut free from all bondage to drugs, drink, pornography, etc.

The celebrant then leads the congregation in prayers of thanks and praise.

> Lord, we bless you that you have overcome the world;
>
> we praise you, Lord, because you have set us free.

The congregation should be encouraged to visualize the Lord standing in its midst, cutting each person free. And those who have been in bondage of any kind should be encouraged to go as soon as they can and celebrate the great sacrament of reconciliation. People coming to confession after this prayer for spiritual healing often have the freedom to bring their whole life into the presence of the all-forgiving Lord.

This is an important prayer and faith experience because it confronts the area of the person's greatest weakness with the power of Jesus Christ. We are not saying to a person struggling with some great burden, "Do the best you can." We are proclaiming to that person that Jesus has triumphed over all evil, and that there is no evil in this person's life over which he will not triumph. Nothing can withstand the power of the Lord. But the person must repent and believe. If the person clings to any kind of sinful desire the Lord cannot free him or her. Very often the real significance of this prayer experience is that it shows the person, perhaps for the first time, the possibility of being freed.

So often people do not bring their addictions or the addictions of their loved ones to the Lord. Months after a healing service I received a letter from a lady in which she wrote:

> I asked your blessing for my daughter who was in the control of an evil woman. I now know that that very night she was set free.

Her daughter was in Brazil. The mother became convinced during the prayer that the Lord would set her daughter free, and when she came to me for personal prayer she simply asked me to pray too. Together, in the name of Jesus, we commanded that the evil bondage be broken. The daughter wrote that she had left the house—on the very night we were praying—and had broken off the lesbian relationship.

A priest was living in great fear of his homosexual urges. When I prayed with him for spiritual healing, he was completely set free. Afterward he told me that I should proclaim to the whole world that Jesus frees the homosexual.

Jesus has given us his own authority to combat the powers of evil in his name and set people free. If we do not use that authority, if we presume there is nothing we can do in a situation, our whole Christian ministry is undermined. Although that girl in Brazil was thousands of miles away, her mother's faith and love spanned the distance and we could pray for her as confidently as if she had been present with us in the church.

People caught in the bondage of drugs, alcohol, sexual abuse or the many forms of the occult need more than compassion and understanding—they need someone to bring into their lives the power of Jesus Christ. They need ministry in the name of Jesus. Moralizing is not enough; exhortation is not enough; forebearance is not enough. The Christian cannot be satisfied with anything less than total freedom in the name of Jesus.

A person may only gradually realize a spiritual healing. A friend was suffering deeply from depression and came to stay in our community. She attended all the prayers for healing of memories and healing of relationships, yet the depression remained.

> I began to feel again God's love for me. I was making a great effort, but I was still depressed. I had a terrible tension in my stomach and I could not eat. I told Father about it and he said it was resentment. I knelt down and he prayed in the name of Jesus that I would be released from this resentment. It is difficult to express in words what happened. It was as if something had burst or melted inside me. A weight lifted from me. . . . Four days later I saw the doctor and he said that I was out of depression. I saw him again one month later and he discharged me.

The prayer of command in the name of Jesus is sometimes the only way to free a person. Priests should be very aware of this power in their daily ministry. If prayer for the healing of memories and the healing of relationships has not brought freedom to the sufferer, then we should pray for spiritual healing. The root may be some form of bondage. We can break that bondage through the power of Christ.

Normally, in a healing service, I spend only about five minutes in the prayer for spiritual healing. In the

prayer for the healing of relationships we have asked
the Lord to heal within us all pride and arrogance, and
we have invited the Holy Spirit to come into the area
of our weakness. Now it is sufficient to confront evil
with the power of Jesus and command it to go. We
should encourage people who are in bondage to come
to the sacraments and celebrate God's mercy. Very
often people who have been touched by the healing
service will be anxious to come back to the sacraments.

Physical Healing

We now pray for physical healing. Through the
preceding prayers for inner healing people not only
have experienced healing, but they also have received
an important teaching on the meaning and nature of
healing. They now know more clearly that physical
healing is only one type of healing, and not the most
important type. And yet, for the person who is suffering some ailment, physical healing is very important.
Sick people, people who may have been away from
church for many years, will come to the healing service. They want healing. We center this prayer too in
the Eucharist, pointing out how frequently we pray for
healing in the Mass. With a Catholic congregation it is
always helpful to center this prayer and every prayer
for healing in the Mass. This encourages them to ask
with a more expectant faith. A simple prayer of praise
and petition is addressed to the Lord:

> Lord Jesus, we bless you that while you walked this
> earth you had compassion on the sick and you
> healed them. And we thank you, Lord, that you
> commissioned your disciples to do likewise in your
> name. Lord, we ask you to send your healing Spirit
> into our weak bodies; free us, Lord, from all pain
> and sickness and grant us health of body, mind and

spirit, so that we may rejoice in your service. You are Lord for ever and ever.

We have to encourage people to invite the Spirit to enter into the area of their pain and sickness. As the Spirit enters their weakness he will either heal them physically or give them the grace to endure which he gave to St. Paul:

> My grace is all you need, for my power is strongest when you are weak (2 Cor 12:9).

Having opened his or her life to the Lord in the prayer for the healing of memories and relationships, the person is now well-disposed to confidently ask the Lord for health of mind and body and to praise God if he or she is not blessed with a return to physical health. The inner peace which the sick receive through forgiving everyone and through being freed from all inner resentment and bitterness gives them the strength to face a life of physical sickness or disability with great courage. As they receive this deep peace of soul and enter into the complete acceptance of God's plan in their life, great healing takes place. One woman who was suffering great distress through multiple sclerosis attended a healing service and afterward wrote:

> Thank you! How else can I put it, as since last Tuesday I have been out of tremendous pain, and after being able to see out of a part of my left eye only, I can now, at times, see completely, which is wonderful. But what to me is more wonderful than all that is the fact that the kind gentleman who brought me, because of my husband's bout of flu, honestly admits that for 36 years he disbelieved in God only to find that on last Tuesday his thoughts were in turmoil. Now he is starting to read the Good News.

Her eyesight was completely restored and later on the

doctor took her off the pills which she had been taking for 30 years. And the man who brought her to the service has become a faithful communicant in his Anglican parish. The woman who was healed physically rejoiced more in the gift of faith which he received than in her own healing.

This particular case has taught me many things about the power the Lord gives to the church to bear witness to him. The woman, who was almost blind physically, was brought to the service by a man who was spiritually blind. He volunteered to bring her because, as he said, "I have nothing to fear from that kind of thing!" During the service he found faith. It wasn't the teaching which enlightened him. He was overcome by the witness of a praying community—everyone praising God and acknowledging the presence of the risen Lord. God ceased to be an idea, which he could deny, and became a presence, which he could not deny. This was St. Paul's method of evangelization.

> When I came to you, I was weak and trembled all over with fear, and my teaching and message were not delivered with skillful words of human wisdom, but with convincing proof of the power of God's Spirit. Your faith, then, does not rest on human wisdom but on God's power (1 Cor 2:3-5).

The healing service, which we really should call a service of prayer for healing, is a celebration of the word of God and provides people with an experience of the power of God. Faith, as St. Paul says, "does not rest on human wisdom, but on God's power." If faith is not resting on God's power, God becomes a very distant Father, if not just a vague idea. People need to know the presence of God; they need to experience his power in their own lives and witness his Spirit at work in the church. Ideas convert nobody.

Praying for healing is a manifestation of the power of God, because God alone can heal. The preacher who proclaims the healing love of God, but refuses to pray for healing is not really bearing witness to the message. Preaching is always more than words. Preaching must be a witness to the message and a demonstration of the truth of the message. The healing service provides a good opportunity to preach the gospel with power and complete conviction. There is a very intimate relationship between preaching conversion and praying for healing. Preaching without healing is powerless; healing without preaching, meaningless. In the prayer for healing we are demonstrating our own faith in God's promise, and it is this witness which gives power to our preaching.

The Oil of Gladness

We conclude the healing service with an anointing with blessed oil, which is often called the oil of gladness. This is a very fitting title because joy is truly the fruit of this anointing. People return to their homes glad in heart, with the joy of the Spirit.

The difference between the oil of gladness and the oil used in the sacrament of the sick must be explained to the people. This anointing is not a sacrament, it is a sacramental. Our faith is a sacramental faith. God always uses signs and symbols to speak to us. He has given us the sacraments—clear, unambiguous signs of his redeeming presence. The church also sets aside blessed objects to serve as sacramentals—physical, tangible, visible, blessed by the church as a support for our faith. God's blessing and God's presence is mediated to us through things.

> There is no good trying to be more spiritual than
> God. God never meant man to be a purely spiritual
> creature. That is why He uses material things like
> bread and wine to put new life into us. We may
> think this rather crude and unspiritual. God does
> not: He invented eating. He likes matter. He in-
> vented it.[3]

The blessing of oil for use by the laity is a very ancient
sacramental. In the Roman Ritual we have this blessing:

> Our help is in the name of the Lord.
> *Response:* Who made heaven and earth.
>
> God's creature, oil,
> I cast out the demon from you
> by God the Father almighty +
> who made heaven and earth and sea
> and all that they contain.
> Let the adversary's power, the devil's legions,
> and all Satan's attacks and machinations
> be dispelled and driven afar from this creature oil.
> Let it bring health in body
> and mind to all who use it,
> in the name of God +, the Father almighty,
> and of our Lord Jesus Christ +, his Son, and of the
> Holy Spirit +, the Advocate,
> as well as in the love of the same
> Jesus Christ our Lord,
> who is coming to judge both the living
> and the dead
> and the world by fire. Amen.
>
> Lord hear my prayer.
> *Response:* And let my cry be heard by you.
> The Lord be with you.
> *Response:* And also with you.
>
> Let us pray

C. S. Lewis, *Mere Christianity* (New York: Macmillan, 1964).

Lord God almighty,
before whom the hosts of angels stand in awe
and whose heavenly service we acknowledge,
may it please you to regard favorably
and to bless and hallow this creature, oil,
which by your power has been pressed
from the juice of olives.

You have ordained it for anointing the sick, so that,
    when they are made well, they may give thanks to
    you,
the living and true God.

Grant, we pray, that those who use this oil,
which we are blessing + in your name,
may be delivered from all suffering, all infirmity,
and all the wiles of the enemy.

Let it be a means of averting any kind of adversity
    from man,
made in your image and redeemed by the precious
    blood of your Son,
so that he may never again suffer
the sting of the ancient serpent,
through Christ our Lord. Amen.

(The oil is sprinkled with holy water)[4]

The priest may use this ancient blessing of the Roman
Ritual, or he may use one of his own choice.

The people show by their eagerness to receive the
blessing that they understand the significance of this
sacramental. Having prayed for healing and opened
their whole lives to the Spirit, they now present
themselves for an individual blessing. As people come
forward to receive the blessing, the congregation sings
and, what is most striking, keeps singing until the last
person has been blessed. With a large congregation—perhaps a thousand people—this may take one
or two hours, depending on the number of ministers

4 *Roman Ritual*, trans. Philip Weller (Milwaukee: Bruce, 1964).

available. On our Redemptorist parish missions we often begin with the healing service. The congregation stays in the church singing and praising God for three hours if necessary. People want to be blessed, and they will wait, prayerfully, for the blessing.

The blessing with oil is a very intimate, private moment when the person may ask for a specific grace or healing. Usually people ask for inner healing, especially within the marriage and the family. When a whole family comes forward marvelous healing of relationships takes place. If the family members are not all present, it is very important for husband and wife to come forward together. Their marriage will be renewed as they ask together for healing.

On one occasion a venerable priest, who was judiciously making up his mind about the whole thing, was approached by a woman who asked him to bless her and pray for God to forgive her for her hatred of the Catholic church. God had healed her of that hatred during the service. All the priest's doubts were resolved!

During an ecumenical healing retreat which I conducted in a top security prison in London, the healing service was a most blessed occasion. Men with very bitter memories found deep peace in the Lord. One prisoner described the anointing in a letter to his parish priest:

> The final part was the anointing with the oil of gladness. Yes, we were anointed with the oil of gladness on our forehead and hands. Each of the four chaplains plus Father Jim performed the anointing as lines of men went up to be anointed. We asked for special intentions and for healing in ourselves and/or for others. I prayed for a moment or two with chaplain and returned to my place. Hymns of praise and thanksgiving were being sung throughout. It was beautiful.

The following night in the prison we had another service of prayer for healing and the outpouring of the Holy Spirit. The same prisoner wrote:

> How can I express in words the experience of Sunday evening? We gathered and prayed for the gift of the Holy Spirit in words and singing continuously. It was an experience of great joy. We prayed collectively for the gift of the Spirit for ourselves. Then we went individually to be prayed with. There was a continuous stream of people going up. Everyone was joyfully singing or praying. I could see great joy on the faces of everyone. It was out of this world.

The blessing with oil and the prayer for the release of the Spirit has this effect on people. They come forward for it with great expectation, and they are not disappointed. Those prisoners, many of whom were serving life sentences for very serious crimes, had a profound experience of the healing presence of the Lord through the anointing. I have asked myself since what I would have done for those men if I hadn't conducted the healing service on Saturday and prayed for the outpouring of the Spirit on Sunday. How would they have come into an experience of the risen Lord? How would they have experienced the joy which they all experienced?

If people are not brought into an experience of the risen Lord in their midst, preaching is empty and hearts remain unmoved. The healing service, and especially the anointing with the blessed oil, provides the occasion for people to have a most powerful experience of the Lord. It is that experience, that touch of the Lord, which binds up the broken heart.

CHAPTER EIGHT:
The Intercessory Role of Mary

The powerful intercession of Mary, the mother of God, has always been sought in times of sickness and trouble. Faith in the efficacy of her intercession is manifested in prayers from the earliest ages of the church. A prayer written in Greek on a fragment of a third-century papyrus expressed this faith. It is still prayed today:

> We fly to thy patronage, O Holy Mother of God. Despise not our petitions in our necessities, but deliver us from all danger, O ever glorious and blessed Virgin.

We ask our Lady to "deliver us," applying to her the same words used in the Lord's Prayer when we say "deliver us from evil."

The church's confidence in Mary's intercession comes from experience. Under the guidance of the Holy Spirit the church very quickly realized that the words which Jesus spoke on Calvary to his mother and his disciple John were addressed to us all: "He is your son. . . . She is your mother."

In the scriptures we see Mary as a woman most obedient to the word of God. She pondered the word in her heart. She lived by the word and acted by the word. When the angel announced to her that she would bear a son through the power of the Holy Spirit, she replied, "May it happen to me as you have said." And through the power of that word of God Mary became the mother of the Son of God. She became the mother of the physical, historical Jesus Christ. Again the word of God was spoken to her, this time from the cross: "He is your son." And through the power of that word of God, spoken by Jesus, she became the mother not only of John, but of all disciples.

> This maternity of Mary in the order of grace began with the consent which she gave in faith at the Annunciation and which she sustained without wavering beneath the cross. This maternity will last - without interruption until the eternal fulfillment of all the elect. For, taken up to heaven, she did not lay aside this saving role, but by her manifold acts of intercession continues to win for us gifts of eternal salvation (*Dogmatic Constitution on the Church*, No. 62).

Because of her relationship with Jesus, Mary has played an indispensable role in the plan of God. She was chosen by God the Father to be most intimately related to the divine Persons in their redeeming work. The Father chose her to be the mother of his only Son; the Son chose to be born as man from her womb; and the Holy Spirit overshadowed her and produced in her God's greatest creation, the humanity of God, Jesus Christ. The church, guided by the Holy Spirit, has always pondered the depth of this mystery, and the Holy Spirit has led the church to recognize Mary's subordinate role in the work of salvation accomplished by her Son.

The Council says the church experiences the power of Mary's intercession. We find this experience in the lives of the faithful. We see this experience enshrined in the prayers to Mary which have come down through the centuries, for example, in the well-known *Memorare*:

> Remember, O most gracious Virgin Mary, that never was it known that anyone who fled to your protection, implored your help, or sought your intercession, was left unaided. Inspired with this confidence, I fly to you, O Virgin of virgins, my Mother. To you I come, before you I stand, sinful and sorrowful. O Mother of the Word Incarnate! Despise not my petitions, but in your mercy hear and answer me. Amen.

This prayer has lived throughout many centuries in the hearts of the faithful because it expresses how the faithful have experienced the powerful intercession of Mary. If the extraordinary confidence in Mary embodied in this prayer found no resonance in the heart, the faithful would never have treasured this prayer and handed it on. The same is true of the beautiful *Salve Regina*:

> Hail, holy Queen, Mother of Mercy, our life, our sweetness, and our hope! To you we cry, poor banished children of Eve; to you we send up our sighs, mourning and weeping in this valley of tears. Turn then, O most gracious advocate, your eyes of mercy toward us, and after this our exile, show unto us the blessed fruit of your womb, Jesus. O clement, O loving, O sweet Virgin Mary.

This prayer has been part of the church's liturgy of night prayer, or Compline, for centuries.

Throughout the year, the church's liturgy keeps the powerful intercession of Mary before us. Speaking of the renewed General Calendar of the liturgical year Pope Paul VI wrote:

This calendar is arranged in such a way as to give fitting prominence to the celebration on appropriate days of the work of salvation. It distributes throughout the year the whole mystery of Christ, from the Incarnation to the expectation of His return in glory, and thus makes it possible to include, in a more organic and closely-knit fashion, the commemoration of Christ's Mother in the annual cycle of mysteries of her Son (*Marialis Cultus*, No. 2).

In Advent, for instance, we celebrate the Immaculate Conception; during the Christmas season, on New Year's Day, we have the solemnity of Mary, Mother of God. On March 25 we celebrate the Annunciation, and on August 15, the Assumption. The memorial of the Queenship of the Blessed Virgin Mary is August 22. These feasts are celebrations of the main dogmatic truths concerning our Lady. But we have several other important feasts as well: September 8, the Birth of Our Lady; May 31, Visitation; September 15, Our Lady of Sorrows; February 11, Our Lady of Lourdes; July 16, Our Lady of Mount Carmel; and October 7, Our Lady of the Rosary. And, of course, there are many local and regional feasts in honor of Mary.

These feasts and commemorations of our Lady in the liturgy keep the example of Mary, the humble virgin, before our eyes, and through the purity of heart, which is so manifest in Mary, our sinful hearts are lifted up in expectation of a greater purification. In the liturgy, Mary is commemorated as our mother in whom the grace of redemption is complete. She teaches us how to rejoice in God, our savior. Joy comes through purity of heart. The impure heart cannot rejoice. The gift of joy, the grace of rejoicing, brings healing to the heart. Until God alone becomes the source of our joy, the heart remains divided and the sadness of sin, rooted in pride, remains. The humble heart learns from Mary how to rejoice in its lowliness. While liturgical devotion to Mary keeps our minds fixed on the great truths of Christ, on his incarnation, death and resurrection, it also keeps our hearts fixed on the gospel response to these mysteries, on purity of heart and humility of spirit. On the Saturday following the second Sunday after Pentecost we commemorate the Immaculate Heart of Mary. We pray for the grace of purification:

> Father,
> you prepared the heart of the Virgin Mary
> to be a fitting home for your Holy Spirit.
> By her prayers
> may we become a more worthy temple of your glory
> (*Opening Prayer*).

Later in the Mass, we pray that we may rejoice:

> Lord,
> you have given us the sacrament of eternal
> redemption.
> May we who honor the mother of your Son
> rejoice in the abundance of your blessings
> and experience the deepening of your life within us
> (*Prayer after Communion*).

As we honor our Lady in the liturgy we are led, step by step, to pray for a greater purity of heart, for the grace to rejoice in God and, finally, for the grace to experience the new life of Christ within us. Whenever the church contemplates Mary, the sinless virgin, she prays for joy. And she prays for God to protect us from all those things which would oppose or destroy joy.

The following testimony illustrates how devotion to Mary brings the gift of joy and deep inner healing. The writer is a 32-year-old woman.

All my life I have cried uncontrollable tears of deep sadness. It was as if the sadness of the world was inside me! This blocked every channel of growth in me, and the awareness of my inability to control it was a source of great distress. Then someone introduced me to the Rosary. He talked about Mary with such conviction of her power and love, explaining that she was my mother and loved me very much.

I started to say the Rosary. I immediately found a comfort, consolation and peace that I had never experienced before. Saying the Rosary now is not only easy—it has become a hunger. I find I am always using it to pray for other people and the results have been miraculous. It is through our Lady that I have been able to give Jesus to others. And, although I had been praying for many years for Jesus to take away this sadness, it was only while praying to our Lady for others that my prayer has been answered without even asking.

I know now that even though I have always loved Jesus and had been close to him, he wanted so much to give me his mother that I was to progress no further in life until I knew her as my mother also. The circumstances of my life are much the same, but I am now pervaded by an inner joy and happiness. The Rosary has now become so much part of my life that I could not live without it.

This woman was healed of a deep sadness through the Rosary—and notice that it was while saying the Rosary for others! The power of the Rosary can also be seen in the following incident. In her eightieth year my mother was very upset by something that happened. When I heard about it, I called and asked how she was coping. She replied, "Oh, I am all right now, but it took two Rosaries to get rid of it." She brought the wound she had received to the contemplation of the mysteries of Christ in the Rosary, and as she prayed, she was healed. Instead of giving in to self-pity, or criticizing what had happened, she meditated on the mysteries of Christ and was set free. This is the great value of the Rosary as a form of prayer. It brings us into the contemplation of Christ immediately. It is impossible to contemplate the scourging at the pillar or the crowning with thorns, for example, and hold on to self-pity!

As we contemplate the mysteries of the Rosary, our whole being is immersed in the mystery of Christ, in his incarnation, death and resurrection, and from this immersion we emerge refreshed, healed and renewed. But we must enter into the mystery in prayerful contemplation. We should never rush this prayer. Pope Paul VI talks about the need for a "lingering pace" in saying the Rosary. We must have time to hold on to certain scenes and words. He writes:

> By its nature the recitation of the Rosary calls for a quiet rhythm and a lingering pace, helping the individual to meditate on the mysteries of the Lord's life as grasped by the heart of her who was closer to the Lord than all the others. In this way the unfathomable riches of these mysteries are unfolded (*Marialis Cultus*, No. 47).

There is no sickness, nor sin, nor inner wound which we cannot bring to the Rosary. The Christ whom we contemplate is the Christ who is dying for our sins. As we contemplate his love on the cross the barriers of sin are destroyed. The Christ whom we contemplate in the incarnation has come "that we may have life and have it in abundance"; as we contemplate Christ coming into this world to bring us abundant life, we can more calmly face sickness and death. The Christ we meet in the Rosary blesses us with his gift of peace. As we open our hearts to receive his peace, our inner wounds are healed. Devotion to Mary, particularly devotion to the Rosary, is a sure way to the contemplation of Jesus through whose wounds we have been healed. To the person with a devotion of our Lady the words of Jesus, "She is your Mother," are the life-giving word of God. He lives by that word.

APPENDIX:
Healing the Self-Image Through Personal Prayer

There is a marked discrepancy between the revealed truth that we are made in the image of God and the way we feel about ourselves. The way we feel about ourselves is what we call our self-image. Or rather, we should say the self-image determines the way we feel about ourselves. Have you ever tried to describe how you feel about yourself? Allen Wheelis, the famous psychiatrist quoted in Chapter 7, describes feeling overcome by his negative self-image:

> It is late at night. I feel a strange unease. The room is so quiet, the hum of a clock is the roar of a distant ocean, a tide of people and events washing on other shores, passing me by. I feel unworthy, remember times when I have been angry with this or that person. How strange! I cannot now imagine being angry at anyone. I feel undeserving, I should be grateful just to be alive, overwhelmed if anyone should like me, if a patient should find me helpful, am dismayed to recall moments of intolerance, of criticalness. Who am I to set standards of conduct, to pass judgment on anyone? Suddenly I cannot bear the silence.[1]

[1] Wheelis, op. cit.

No one is born with a poor self-image. The self-image is shaped and formed as we develop by the things that happen to us, and especially by the words that are spoken to us. A word is very powerful. A word can destroy or it can give life.

Ultimately we have to say that the self-image is formed around the creative word of God or around the destructive word of the world. If we want to know who we are and what kind of a person we are, we should ask God. It is God who made us and he alone knows us through and through. Not only is our self-image formed by a word, but we will live by that word. Jesus tells us to live by every word that comes from the mouth of God. If we allow God's word to form our self-image, we will be able to live by the word of God. On the other hand, if we allow the word of the world to form our self-image, we will live by the word of the world.

The healing of the self-image comes through listening to the word of God. This listening involves three steps: acceptance, acknowledgment, and allowance. Healing will be experienced as we pray our way through these three steps.

Acceptance

Our first response to the word of God is to accept it. Acceptance of the word of God is not merely an intellectual assent. Acceptance involves total immersion in the word. Jesus said:

> "If you make my word your home
> you will indeed be my disciples,
> you will learn the truth
> and the truth will make you free" (Jn 8:31-32,
> Jerusalem Bible).

Notice the progression toward freedom. The first step is to make the word of Jesus our home. Home is the place where we can relax and feel accepted and loved. We must be at home in the word of God. We must enter into the word and dwell in it. When we dwell comfortably in the word, we will be able to take the second step on the road to freedom: becoming disciples.

A disciple is one who listens to the master, who learns from the master, and who seeks in every way to be like the master. When we have become disciples by making the word our home, we will be ready for the third step: freedom. We will know the truth. By dwelling within the word of God we learn God's truth about ourselves. Jesus reveals who each disciple is in relation to himself or herself, and in relation to God the Father and God the Holy Spirit. That is the truth which we must learn. It is that truth alone which sets us free.

Before we can speak the liberating word of truth, we must learn it as disciples, learn it as we dwell prayerfully within the word of God. Too often we speak instead a binding word, a word that hurts and wounds and destroys.

The first step, then, in listening to God is to accept his word, to enter into his word and make our home in it, and then in the power of this word of truth about ourselves to deny the word of untruth spoken by the world, the flesh and the devil. If we do not accept the word about ourselves which God speaks to us, we will certainly accept the word which the world speaks. What word does God speak to us? He says, "You are precious to me" (Ps 43:4).

In our prayer we accept this word that we are precious in God's sight. We enter into this word and give God thanks and praise. The sign of our acceptance of this word of God about ourselves is our ability to thank God for the wonder of our being. This response is the first step in prayer for the healing of the self-image. We musn't rush it. We must hear God speak his word, his creative, life-giving word in the depths of our being—"You are precious to me"—and then, in the presence of God, we must respond with thanks. We must begin to live by this word. When we feel bad about something we will simply pray,

> I thank you for my being.
> I praise you that I am precious to you.

instead of yielding to feelings of self-destruction and self-pity.

People who spend five minutes in the morning praising God for the wonder of their being will have no problem in coping with attacks on their self-image during the day. I always ask those who are suffering from a poor self-image to spend at least five minutes hearing the word that they are precious to God and responding to it with praise and thanks. So many people don't feel precious to God or to anyone else! They are depressed with sadness and loneliness; they fear that nobody will ever love them. They feel like this because they do not love themselves. Self-acceptance, true self-love, is a grace given to us when we accept God's word about ourselves. As Leanne Payne writes:

> To know ourselves at all is to begin to be healed of effects of the Fall, for it involves a coming into a listening-speaking relationship to God. It is to recapture at least to some extent, the Edenic situation. It is to realize more perfectly our union and communion with God. No small thing indeed, but it is our inheritance (and a neglected one) as Christians. It is the healing of our primal loneliness.[2]

[2] Leanne Payne, *The Broken Image* (Westchester, IL: Good News, 1981).

Self-acceptance is possible only in the light of the word of God. We hear God's word declaring that we are precious to him, and we respond to it with praise and thanks. As we say in the second eucharistic prayer,

> We thank you for counting us worthy
> to stand in your presence and serve you.

We form our self-image around this affirming word of God, and in the power of this word of God we face all the other words that come at us from the world.

When we have truly accepted the word of God about ourselves, the word that declares that we are precious to God, we then, in prayer, accept that word of others. We bring before the Lord the people with whom we share our lives, and we praise God that they too are precious in his sight. It is very important for us to bring before the Lord in this way anyone who is causing us some problem. It is important to mention each person by name, in the presence of God, and accept the person as God's precious creation. If someone has upset us, it will be difficult for us to see that person in a good light. Hence the need to see him or her in the light of the word of God. We may be sad and depressed because someone has offended us, and we can no longer relate to that person. We feel hurt and let down. When we think of the person all those hurt feelings begin to come up. The temptation, then, is to repress the feelings, to pretend that they are not there. Instead of repressing the hurt feelings, we should bring them into the presence of God and praise God for the person who hurt our feelings. As we praise God for that person, as we acknowledge that that person is precious to God, our hurt feelings begin to experience healing. We may be angry, but instead of letting the anger become aggressive or abusive, we admit that we are angry and thank God for those with whom we are angry. It is impossible to say, "Lord, I bless you for Peter, who has hurt me," and continue to hold on to resentment against him. This is a very effective healing prayer.

When someone hurts us, our image of that person changes. If we live with the changed image, we continue to hold on to resentment. But when we praise God that this person is precious in his sight, we begin, once again, to see the person as God sees him or her. We can see the person either through the hurt we have experienced—and then we will have a very bad view—or we can see the person through the light of the word of God.

We have two steps to take in the prayer of acceptance. We must accept the word of God which declares that each person is precious in his sight, and then we must accept the same word of God which declares that the person who has offended us is also precious in the sight of God. A few minutes of prayer in the morning along these lines will not only bring healing to our self-image, but healing to our view of other people as well.

Acknowledgment

The second step in listening to God is to acknowledge what God is doing in us. Our Lady, because she knew how to ponder the word of God, could acknowledge that the Lord had done great things for her, and so she could rejoice in God, her Savior. Acknowledging with joy and gratitude all the good things that God does in our lives is a prerequisite for healing. What is good in our lives is God's gift. Anything within us which refuses to bless the name of God is either a sin or the wound of sin.

As we acknowledge God at work in our lives we

should also listen to hear God acknowledge us as his children. After Jesus was baptized the heavens opened and the Spirit of God came down upon him and the Father acknowledged him with the words,

"You are my own dear Son. I am pleased with you."

Spiritually speaking, the sky has opened over each one of us and the Spirit of the Lord has come upon us and the Father has acknowledged us as his children. We should listen to hear those words of the Father: "You are my beloved son (daughter). I am pleased with you." Jesus needed that word of acknowledgment—so do we. If we do not listen for the word of acknowledgment which the Father speaks for our encouragement, we will become victims of the destructive word which the world speaks.

When we acknowledge in prayer all the good things the Lord is doing in us, we then acknowledge what he is doing in others. We have seen how important it is, and how healing it is, to accept that others are precious in the sight of God. Now we develop that acceptance, and we begin to acknowledge what God is doing in their lives. If we don't praise God for what he is doing in others, we will become jealous of them and their successes will begin to deprive us of our peace. The sure sign of jealousy is the inability to acknowledge that someone has done a good job. This prayer of acknowledgment is the best way to deal with jealousy. It is impossible to remain jealous while acknowledging the good things God is doing in another person. As we acknowledge what God is doing in another, our image of that person is transformed. We begin to see him or her as a collaborator with God. If the person has hurt us in any way, this prayer of acknowledgment brings a deep and lasting healing.

Each morning we should take a few moments to acknowledge what God is doing in our lives, and then to acknowledge what he is doing in the lives of the people with whom we will share our work and time during the day.

Allowance

The third step in listening to God is to make allowance for our own sinfulness. As we become aware of who we are in the presence of God, aware that we are precious in God's sight, we also become aware of our sinfulness. As we confess our sinfulness to the Lord, we make our home in his word of forgiveness:

> The Lord is merciful and loving,
>   slow to become angry and full of constant love.
> He does not keep on rebuking;
>   he is not angry for ever.
> He does not punish us as we deserve. . . .
>
> As far as the east is from the west
>   so far does he remove our sins from us.
> As a father is kind to his children,
>   so the LORD is kind to those who honor him.
> He knows what we are made of;
>   he remembers that we are dust (Ps 103:8-10, 12-14).

We must learn to make allowance for all our own weaknesses, and in the presence of God we must forgive ourselves. Forgiveness is God's gift which we must share with others. But to share it effectively with others, we must know how to receive it for ourselves. We must extend to ourselves the same unconditional forgiveness which we know we must extend to others. If we do not take this step and positively forgive ourselves, we will remain guilty in the presence of God and, as a consequence, we will be reluctant to enter into his presence.

Sorrow for sin is not disappointment with self! We ask God's pardon for our sins, and then we forgive ourselves. As we learn to make allowance for ourselves, in the presence of God, we also learn how to make allowance for others. We forgive others "seventy times seven." If we do not take this step of making allowance for ourselves and others, our listening to God will be disturbed either by a guilty sense of our own sinfulness or by the remembrance of the sins and offenses of others. By forgiving ourselves and others, we enter into a deeper peace in the presence of God and are able to hear the word of God with a new clarity.

When we make allowance for ourselves and for others, we are living a life of divine wisdom. A humble and contrite heart you will not despise, O Lord!